PERSONAL FINANCE & PROPERTY MASTERY HACKS

Supercharge Your Finances With Tax Savings, Generate Revenue From Your Real Estate And Maximize Your Income Through Strategic Relocation

WILLIAM DAVIS

CONTENTS

INTRODUCTION

Welcome to a journey that promises to revolutionize your financial future. Imagine the possibility of transforming your financial situation not just through traditional means but by considering the untapped potential of strategic relocation. My hack of "Moving for Money" is a game-changer in the realm of financial management.

What if I told you that you could save thousands of dollars simply by moving a mile down the road? For some, this may be the case. Moving out of the city limits could save you several percent in income taxes and the city limits may be less than a mile away. Imagine the extra money you could keep in your pocket! With the soaring inflation today and the increasing taxes, it is more important than ever to be actively looking for ways to save or generate more money and it's crucial to seek innovative ways to bolster your financial standing.

As someone who has experienced the ups and downs of personal finance, I understand the journey to economic stability can be challenging. My professional career has given me unique insights into the financial benefits of relocating for work. I have successfully navigated the complexities of personal finance and have discovered practical and powerful strategies that can make a significant difference in anyone's financial journey. This book is my way of sharing these insights to empower you to take control of your finances in practical and effective ways you might not have considered before.

The concept that moving can dramatically enhance your financial situation may seem unconventional, but it's a strategy that can lead to significant and transformative results. By relocating to areas with lower taxes, cost of living, and better job opportunities, you can maximize your income and minimize your expenses, paving the way for a more financially secure future. This book is about opening your eyes to the financial revolution that comes with strategic relocation, coupled with intelligent financial management, and the exciting possibilities it can bring.

My journey from financial uncertainty to stability has been fueled by strategic moves and sound financial practices. Moving for job opportunities and leveraging the financial benefits of different locations have played a crucial role in my success. My experience in real estate investment and financial planning has equipped me with the tools to help others achieve similar success. I am passionate about personal finance and believe that anyone, regardless of their current financial situation, can achieve financial freedom with the proper knowledge and strategies.

This book aims to transform the financial lives of individuals across all income levels by introducing innovative saving and earning strategies. Whether you are struggling with debt, looking to save more, or seeking ways to increase your income, this book offers practical, actionable steps tailored for you. The target audience includes those eager to improve their financial literacy and those ready to take bold steps to enhance their financial well-being.

What sets "Personal Finance & Property Mastery Hacks" apart from other personal finance guides is its unique approach to combining financial management with strategic relocation. This novel perspective demonstrates how moving can be a powerful tool to optimize your financial situation, offering solutions beyond traditional advice.

The book is structured to guide you through every step of your financial journey. We begin by laying a solid financial foundation, covering essentials like budgeting, debt management, and building an emergency fund. Having a solid base is crucial to your long-term success on your path to prosperity. We then explore advanced personal finance strategies, including tax optimization and investment opportunities. Finally, we examine the benefits of strategic relocation and other innovative ways to maximize income and reduce expenses. It doesn't have to be far away; it could be just down the road. I know you may be thinking that moving down the road isn't as easy as I'm making it sound, but we'll also cover how to overcome any obstacles that might be in your way. When you're ready to act, be sure to plan it out and take advantage of all the resources at your fingertips. This book is designed to help you navigate through any hurdles, equipping you with the knowledge and strategies to make your transition smooth and financially rewarding.

Taking control of your financial destiny is not just a dream—it's an achievable reality. The strategies discussed in this book are practical, proven, and designed to produce real results. You have the power to change your financial future and this book will provide you with the roadmap.

It's natural to have fears and objections when managing personal finances and considering relocation. This book addresses these concerns head-on, providing you with the knowledge and tools to overcome these challenges. You will learn how to navigate financial uncertainties and make informed decisions that will lead to a more secure future.

I have lived in different areas, each with pros and cons. I won't try to persuade you one way or another that you should move. Still, I hope to arm you with all the information you need to make the right choice when deciding where to call home and potentially how to generate extra income. It should be a decision that aligns with your financial and personal goals. This decision can have a profound effect on the amount of money you get to keep from your paycheck and how much you spend when buying goods. You may even be able to generate some extra income for yourself along the way.

Moving for money, what I like to call it, is not just about finding a cheaper place to live. It's about exploring the many ways you can use your move to increase your financial health. Whether you are looking to save money, make money or both, this book will provide you with the tips and tools to achieve your financial goals.

Moving can also be an opportunity to start a new business or pursue a new career path. Maybe you've always wanted to start your own business but haven't been able to afford the high rent or living expenses in your current location or maybe you want to change careers but can't find the right opportunities where you are. By moving to a new location, you can take advantage of new business opportunities, meet new people and expand your professional network. We will provide tips and strategies for building your network, thriving in a new community and adjusting to differences.

I invite you to embark on this financial journey with an open mind and a willingness to implement the strategies discussed. Let this book be your guide to achieving greater financial freedom and stability. Together, we will explore innovative ways to enhance your financial situation and pave the way for a brighter future. Let's get started on this exciting journey towards financial empowerment and success!

UNDERSTANDING YOUR CURRENT FINANCIAL HEALTH

An investment in knowledge pays the best interest.

— BENJAMIN FRANKLIN

E mbarking on a journey to financial health begins with a clear understanding of where you currently stand. This chapter serves as your foundational guide to diagnosing and improving your financial situation. By targeting the elements that shape your financial landscape, we will equip you with the tools and knowledge necessary to navigate your finances with confidence and precision.

DECIPHERING YOUR CREDIT REPORT: BEYOND THE NUMBERS

A credit report is your financial dossier: a detailed record of your credit history curated by credit bureaus. It influences various aspects of your financial life, making an understanding of its contents crucial for maintaining or improving your financial health.

So, what is a credit score? A credit score is a three-digit number typically ranging from 300 to 850, reflecting your creditworthiness based on your credit history. The score is derived from several key components:

- **Payment History (35%)**: This is the most significant factor. It reflects whether you have paid past credit accounts on time. Late payments, bankruptcies, and defaults will lower this score.
- **Amounts Owed (30%)**: This is known as your credit utilization ratio. It considers the total amount you owe and how it compares to your credit limit. Keeping your balances low compared to credit limits is seen as positive.
- **Length of Credit History (15%)**: Longer credit histories are viewed more favorably as they provide more data on your spending habits and repayment behavior.
- **New Credit (10%)**: This includes the number of new accounts you have applied for or opened. Opening several new accounts in a short period can be seen as risky behavior and can lower your score.

- **Types of Credit in Use (10%)**: It can be beneficial to have a mix of account types, such as credit cards, retail accounts, installment loans, finance company accounts, and mortgage loans.

Reading Your Credit Report

Your credit report provides a comprehensive overview of your financial history and is divided into several key sections, each offering unique insights into your creditworthiness. Understanding each section will help you identify areas of improvement and detect potential errors that could negatively impact your credit score.

Personal Information

This section contains your basic identifying information, such as your name, address, Social Security number, and sometimes your employment history. It's essential to verify these details for accuracy. Errors in this section, such as incorrect addresses or unfamiliar employment details, could indicate fraudulent activity or identity theft. Make sure all the information matches your current records.

Credit Accounts

The credit accounts section lists all the accounts you have with various lenders. These include credit cards, auto loans, student loans, mortgages, and other forms of credit. For each account, you'll find details like the type of account, the date it was opened, the credit limit or loan amount, the current balance, and the payment history. Pay close attention to accounts that you do not recognize, as this could suggest unauthorized accounts opened in your name.

Credit Inquiries

Credit inquiries reflect requests made by lenders or other parties to review your credit. These inquiries fall into two categories:

- **Hard Inquiries**: When you apply for new credit (like a credit card or loan), lenders perform a hard inquiry, which can affect your credit score if there are too many in a short period.
- **Soft Inquiries**: These do not impact your score and include checks by companies offering pre-approved credit offers or your requests to review your credit report.

Review these inquiries carefully. If you see hard inquiries that you didn't authorize, it could be a sign of identity theft.

Public Records and Collections

The public records and collections section includes negative financial events like bankruptcies, foreclosures, suits, wage garnishments, liens, and judgments. Collections accounts, typically resulting from unpaid debts, are also listed here. Negative items in this section can have a significant impact on your credit score and remain on your report for seven to ten years, depending on the type of event. Make sure that all information is accurate and up to date.

Identifying Errors

Regularly reviewing your credit report for errors is crucial because inaccuracies can adversely affect your credit score and, consequently, your ability to secure loans or get favorable interest rates. Common errors include outdated information, incorrect account statuses, or unfamiliar accounts that might suggest identity theft.

Steps to Dispute Errors

1. **Write a Dispute Letter**: Report the error in writing to the credit bureau. Identify each mistake, state the facts, and explain why you dispute the information. Request a correction or deletion of the inaccurate data. Include copies (not originals) of any supporting documents.
2. **Send by Certified Mail**: Send your dispute letter by certified mail with a return receipt request so you have a record of when it was delivered.
3. **Follow-Up**: The credit bureau must investigate your dispute within 30 days. If the investigation results in a change to your report, the bureau will send you an updated credit report. Please review it carefully to ensure the errors have been corrected.

By understanding your credit report and proactively identifying errors, you can safeguard your credit score and take control of your financial health.

How does your score impact your financial health? Your credit score affects your ability to secure loans, the interest rates you pay, and your insurance premiums. For instance, a high credit score can help you secure a mortgage at the most competitive interest rates, saving you money over the loan's life. Conversely, a low score can lead to higher interest rates or outright credit rejection.

By understanding how to read and interact with your credit report, you can take proactive steps to improve your financial standing, ensuring you're always in the best position to capitalize on financial opportunities.

BUDGETING BASICS: CREATING YOUR FIRST ZERO-BASED BUDGET

Zero-based budgeting is a powerful and transformative approach to managing your finances. Unlike traditional budgeting methods that only adjust previous spending, zero-based budgeting ensures every dollar you earn is assigned a specific purpose, whether it's covering living expenses, paying off debt, or saving for the future. This meticulous budgeting process not only helps in curbing unnecessary spending but also maximizes your financial efficiency. A great app to use when implementing this approach is Every Dollar App. This is an application usually touted by Dave Ramsey and one that my wife and I use to help with our budgeting.

You can see a big difference when you're not just carelessly whipping out the credit card on a whim and kicking the can down the road to make payments. A zero-based budget requires you to justify every expense and allocate your entire income to various categories, ensuring there is no unassigned money left at the end of the month. This method is crucial for effective financial planning because it provides a comprehensive understanding of where your money is going, allowing for intentional financial decisions rather than habitual spending. It fosters a proactive financial mindset, encouraging you to think critically about each dollar you spend. One thing you might realize is the reality of just how expensive life is in general. I sometimes have found myself wondering where the money went this week, then looking at the Every Dollar app or bank transactions and realizing it was all necessities. When you have a family, things can add up but keeping track of every dollar can help you manage stress by knowing where the money is going.

To create a zero-based budget, follow these steps:

1. **Identify Monthly Income**: Start by calculating your total monthly income from all sources, including salaries, bonuses, and any passive income streams.
2. **List Monthly Expenses**: Write down all your monthly expenses, categorizing them as fixed (like rent or mortgage payments, car payments, insurance) and variable (like groceries, entertainment, and eating out).
3. **Assign Every Dollar a Job**: Allocate every dollar of your income to specific expenses, savings, debt repayment, or investment categories. If there's money left after covering all your essentials, direct it towards financial goals like building an emergency fund or paying off debt faster.
4. **Track and Adjust**: Throughout the month, keep track of your spending and adjust categories as needed. For example, if you underspend in one category, you can redirect the surplus to another category that might need more funding or to a savings goal.

Allocating Every Dollar: The principle of giving every dollar a job is central to zero-based budgeting. This practice not only ensures that you are aware of your spending habits but also prevents wasteful expenditures. Each dollar is treated as a resource that should be optimally utilized, reinforcing the importance of thoughtful spending and saving.

Adjusting As You Go: A zero-based budget is not static; it's a dynamic tool that should evolve with your financial situation. Regular monthly reviews are essential to adjust your budget to better reflect your current financial needs and goals. This might mean changing the allocations based on a raise in income, unexpected expenses, or a change in financial priorities. Such adjustments ensure that your budget remains relevant and continues to work for you in achieving your financial objectives.

Implementing a zero-based budget can be transformative, providing clarity and control over your finances. It encourages a disciplined approach to money management, where every financial decision is deliberate and purposeful. This not only helps in reaching financial goals more efficiently but also instills a lasting habit of fiscal responsibility.

THE EMERGENCY FUND BLUEPRINT: HOW MUCH DO YOU REALLY NEED?

An emergency fund is an essential buffer, safeguarding you against unexpected financial downturns such as medical emergencies, sudden job loss, or urgent home repairs. It is the bedrock of a sound financial plan, providing peace of mind and preventing the need to incur high-interest debt in times of crisis. This section outlines how to determine the right amount for your emergency fund, how to start building it, and where to keep it for both growth and accessibility.

What's the right emergency fund for you? The size of your emergency fund can significantly influence your financial resilience. The general recommendation is to save enough to cover three to six months of living expenses. However, the exact amount depends on several factors, including your job security, health, lifestyle, and family obligations. If you have a stable job and not many dependents, three months might suffice. On the other hand, if your income is variable or you have significant family responsibilities, aiming for six months or more is prudent. I like to try and keep around six months in our family's emergency fund. Having a little extra gives you more peace of mind. Consider the following steps to calculate the precise amount you need:

1. **Assess Your Essential Monthly Expenses**: Sum up all your crucial monthly expenses, including rent or mortgage, utilities, groceries, insurance, and any other necessities.
2. **Multiply by Months**: Decide on the number of months you aim to cover. Multiply your monthly essential expenses by this number to get your emergency fund goal.

Building an emergency fund can seem daunting, especially starting from scratch. However, the key is to start small and be consistent:

1. **Set a Monthly Saving Goal**: Based on your budget, determine a realistic amount you can save each month towards your emergency fund. Even a small amount like $50 or $100 can build up over time.
2. **Automate Your Savings**: Set up an automatic transfer from your checking account to your emergency fund immediately after you receive your paycheck. Automation ensures that you save consistently without having to remember to transfer funds each month.

Where should you keep your fund? The location of your emergency fund is as important as the amount saved. It should be easily accessible but also separate from your regular checking account to avoid temptations to use it. Consider these options:

1. **High-Yield Savings Account**: These accounts offer higher interest rates than regular savings accounts, helping your funds grow while remaining accessible. They are typically available through online banks.
2. **Money Market Accounts** are similar to savings accounts but typically offer higher interest rates and check-writing privileges, which can be convenient for emergency access.
3. **Short-Term CDs or Bonds**: For portions of your emergency fund that you might not need immediately, consider certificates of deposit or bonds with short maturities. These can offer slightly higher returns than savings accounts, though they come with less liquidity. This means you cannot immediately access the money before maturity without getting hit with a fee or losing gains.

There are also psychological benefits to having an emergency fund. An adequately funded emergency fund does more than financially protect you—it also offers significant psychological benefits. Knowing you have a financial cushion can reduce stress and anxiety associated with financial uncertainties. This peace of mind is invaluable, allowing you to focus on other aspects of your life and make rational rather than panic-driven financial decisions.

By understanding the importance of an emergency fund, determining how much you need, and methodically building and storing this fund, you empower yourself to handle life's unexpected events with confidence and stability.

NAVIGATING YOUR DEBT: STRATEGIES FOR PRIORITIZATION AND PAYMENT

Debt can be a significant barrier to achieving financial freedom, but managing it effectively is possible with the right strategies. This section focuses on understanding the various types of debt and implementing practical methods for prioritizing and paying them down efficiently. The goal is not only to reduce debt but also to minimize the interest paid over time, thus freeing up more resources for savings and investments.

There are many different types of debt. Debt typically falls into two categories: secured and unsecured. Secured debts are tied to an asset, such as a mortgage for a home or a car loan and have lower interest rates due to the lower risk to lenders. Unsecured debts, like credit cards and student loans, are not backed by assets and usually carry higher interest rates. Understanding these distinctions is crucial as it affects how you should prioritize their repayment.

Two popular methods for debt repayment are the Debt Snowball and Debt Avalanche methods:

Debt Snowball Method: This method involves paying off your debts from the smallest balance to the largest, regardless of the interest rate. It helps create psychological wins, motivating you to continue paying down debt as each smaller balance is cleared. This is how I have typically attacked debt in the past and been successful. Those little wins compound and motivate you to keep going. YOU CAN DO IT!

Example:

Meet Sarah, a 32-year-old marketing professional. Like many people, Sarah found herself burdened with various forms of debt, including credit card balances, a car loan, and a personal loan. The total debt felt overwhelming, and she struggled to keep up with the minimum payments, let alone make a dent in the principal amounts.

Sarah decided to tackle her debt using the debt snowball method, a strategy where you focus on paying off your smallest debts first while making minimum payments on the larger ones. Here is how she did it:

Step 1: List All Debts from Smallest to Largest

Sarah listed her debts in order from the smallest balance to the largest:

1. **Credit Card A**: $1,200 at 18% interest
2. **Credit Card B**: $3,500 at 20% interest
3. **Car Loan**: $7,200 at 6% interest
4. **Personal Loan**: $10,000 at 12% interest

Step 2: Make Minimum Payments on All Debts Except the Smallest

Sarah made the minimum payments on her car and personal loans while focusing all her extra funds on paying off Credit Card A.

Step 3: Pay as Much as Possible on the Smallest Debt

She analyzed her budget and found she could allocate an extra $200 per month toward her debts. So, she paid the minimum payment plus the additional $200 towards Credit Card A.

Step 4: Move to the Next Debt Once the Smallest is Paid Off

After several months of dedicated payments, Sarah paid off Credit Card A. She then moved on to Credit Card B, using the money she had been paying on Credit Card A plus the minimum payment on Credit Card B.

Step 5: Repeat Until All Debts are Paid Off

Here's how the snowball effect worked for Sarah:

- **Credit Card A**: Paid off in 6 months.
- **Credit Card B**: Paid off in 11 months (after paying off Credit Card A).
- **Car Loan**: With the extra funds now available from paying off both credit cards, Sarah added these to her car loan payments. She paid off the car loan in another 12 months.
- **Personal Loan**: Finally, with the combined payments from the credit cards and car loan, Sarah aggressively tackled her personal loan, paying it off in 18 months.

Total Time to Debt-Free: 47 months (just under four years)

By focusing on the smallest debts first, Sarah experienced quick wins that kept her motivated. The momentum she built helped her stay on track and eventually become debt-free. Now, let's look at the debt avalanche!

Debt Avalanche Method: Contrary to the snowball method, the avalanche method prioritizes debts with the highest interest rates first, moving to those with lower rates. This strategy is financially efficient as it reduces the amount of interest paid over time.

Example:

Let's revisit Sarah, our 32-year-old marketing professional, who initially struggled with various forms of debt. This time, Sarah decides to use the debt avalanche method, which focuses on paying off debts with the highest interest rates first while making minimum payments on the others.

Step 1: List All Debts from Highest to Lowest Interest Rate

Sarah listed her debts in order from the highest interest rate to the lowest:

1. **Credit Card B**: $3,500 at 20% interest
2. **Credit Card A**: $1,200 at 18% interest
3. **Personal Loan**: $10,000 at 12% interest
4. **Car Loan**: $7,200 at 6% interest

Step 2: Make Minimum Payments on All Debts Except the Highest Interest Rate Debt

Sarah made the minimum payments on her car loan, personal loan, and Credit Card A while focusing all her extra funds on paying off Credit Card B.

Step 3: Pay as Much as Possible on the Highest Interest Rate Debt

She analyzed her budget and found she could allocate an extra $200 per month toward her debts. So, she paid the minimum payment plus the additional $200 towards Credit Card B.

Step 4: Move to the Next Debt. Once the Highest Interest Rate Debt is Paid Off

After several months of dedicated payments, Sarah paid off Credit Card B. She then moved on to Credit Card A, using the money she had been paying on Credit Card B plus the minimum payment on Credit Card A.

Step 5: Repeat Until All Debts are Paid Off

Here's how the avalanche effect worked for Sarah:

- **Credit Card B**: Paid off in 11 months.
- **Credit Card A**: Paid off in 4 months (after paying off Credit Card B).
- **Personal Loan**: With the extra funds now available from paying off both credit cards, Sarah added these to her personal loan payments. She paid off the personal loan in another 18 months.
- **Car Loan**: Finally, with the combined payments from the credit cards and personal loan, Sarah aggressively tackled her car loan, paying it off in 14 months.

Total Time to Debt-Free: 47 months (just under four years)

By focusing on the highest interest rates first, Sarah minimized the amount of interest she paid over the life of her loans. Although the initial progress was slower than the debt snowball method, Sarah saved more money in interest payments. Both methods are effective, but the next step is to pick one and put it into action!

When should you consider consolidation or refinancing? Consolidation involves combining multiple debts into a single debt, typically at a lower interest rate. It simplifies the repayment process and can lower monthly payments. Refinancing is similar but usually applies to a single loan, where you replace your existing loan with a new one, often at a lower interest rate. Consider these options if:

- You can secure a lower interest rate.
- You want to simplify monthly payments.
- You need to adjust the monthly payment due to changes in your financial situation.

Staying motivated throughout the debt repayment process is critical. Here are some tips to help maintain your focus and motivation:

- **Set Clear Goals**: Define your debt repayment plan's goals, such as being debt-free within five years or saving a certain amount in interest.
- **Celebrate Milestones**: Recognize and celebrate when you reach significant milestones, such as paying off a credit card or reducing your total debt by 50%.
- **Keep Track of Progress**: Regularly monitoring your debt levels can serve as a motivation booster. Seeing the numbers decrease over time can provide a tangible sense of achievement.

Applying these strategies can help you effectively manage and reduce your debt. This not only improves your financial health but also brings you closer to your long-term financial goals. Remember, the journey to becoming debt-free requires patience, commitment, and a well-thought-out strategy, but the financial and psychological rewards are well worth the effort.

SETTING FINANCIAL GOALS: A ROADMAP TO SUCCESS

Setting financial goals is a crucial step on your journey toward financial health and independence. It's not just about the numbers but about envisioning a life where your finances align with your dreams and values. Whether you're aiming to pay off debt, save for a dream vacation or build wealth for retirement, having a clear roadmap can make all the difference.

What is the importance of setting financial goals? Imagine navigating a new city without a map or GPS—it's challenging, if not impossible, to reach your destination. Financial goals serve as your roadmap, providing direction and purpose to your financial decisions. Without clear goals, it's easy to get lost in the day-to-day grind and feel like you're spinning your wheels. But with well-defined goals, you're more motivated to save, invest and make wise financial decisions. You'll find that your spending aligns more closely with your values, helping you find joy in living within your means. Additionally, you can measure progress, celebrate milestones, and adjust your course as needed.

Knowing your short-term vs. long-term goals is essential. Before diving into the mechanics of goal setting, it's important to differentiate between short-term and long-term goals. Short-term goals are those you can achieve within a year or less. They could include paying off a small debt, building an emergency fund or saving for a holiday trip. Long-term goals require more time, often several years or even decades. Buying a home, funding children's education or retiring comfortably fall into this category. Balancing both types of goals ensures that you're working toward immediate achievements while laying the groundwork for a prosperous future.

What are <u>SMART</u> financial goals? The SMART framework ensures that your goals are well-defined and attainable. Here's how to set SMART goals:

- **Specific**: Clearly define what you want to achieve. Instead of saying, "I want to save money," say, "I want to save $5,000 for an emergency fund."
- **Measurable**: Establish criteria to track your progress. For example, "I will save $400 each month until I reach my goal."
- **Achievable**: Make sure your goal is realistic based on your current finances. Saving $1,000 a month might be too ambitious, but $400 could be attainable.
- **Relevant**: Ensure the goal aligns with your broader life values and aspirations. If your primary value is security, then building an emergency fund should resonate with you.
- **Time-bound**: Set a deadline to create urgency and motivate action. "I will save $5,000 in 12 months" provides a clear timeframe.

Once you've set your goals, it's essential to consistently track progress and adjust them as needed. Using budgeting apps like Mint or You Need a Budget (YNAB) can help you monitor your journey effectively. However, even a simple spreadsheet or notebook can work just as well. Breaking down larger goals into smaller milestones can also help you stay motivated. For instance, if your goal is to pay off $20,000 in debt, setting $5,000 milestones and celebrating each achievement will make the process feel more manageable.

Review your goals at least once a month, celebrate your wins, and identify areas that need adjustment. Life happens and goals may shift accordingly. Recognizing when you need to pivot without losing sight of your ultimate vision is important. Staying flexible while maintaining focus is key.

Feel empowerment through goal setting! It's easy to feel overwhelmed by financial jargon and challenges but setting clear and achievable goals puts the power back in your hands. You're no longer at the mercy of unexpected expenses or mounting debt. Instead, you're taking deliberate steps toward a life of financial security and fulfillment. Embrace the journey and remember that each goal achieved is a victory worth celebrating.

With these foundational strategies in place, you'll not only have a clearer picture of your financial health but also a roadmap guiding you toward a future where your finances are aligned with your values and aspirations.

TAX STRATEGIES

One of the biggest advantages or disadvantages of where you live is going to be the tax rates. This includes city income taxes, school income taxes, state income taxes, property taxes, sales taxes, business income taxes, retirement income taxes and possibly commuter taxes. When you add all these up, where you live can have a massive impact on how much money you get to keep from your paycheck and income! First, we will dive into some of the tax basics and break them down so you understand your bracket and some basic strategies you can use to lower your tax liability. Then we will show you how, where you call home, can affect your bank account. By the end of this chapter, you might find yourself scrolling through Zillow!

UNDERSTANDING YOUR TAX BRACKET AND ITS IMPACT ON YOUR FINANCES

Navigating the world of income taxes can feel like entering a labyrinth, especially with the myriad of forms, rates, and deductions. However, understanding the fundamentals of income tax is crucial for optimizing your tax strategy and keeping more of your hard-earned money. This section is designed to help you understand how tax brackets work and how this knowledge can be utilized to optimize your financial strategies, ultimately affecting your take-home pay and overall financial health.

How do tax brackets work? The United States uses a progressive tax system, which means that as your income increases, the taxes you pay on your income can also increase. However, not all your income is taxed at the same rate due to this system. For instance:

- If you are single and your taxable income is $50,000 in 2024, your first $10,275 is taxed at 10%, the next $31,500 at 12%, and the remaining amount at 22%.

This tiered system ensures that only the income within each bracket is taxed at the corresponding rate, which is a critical point to understand when planning your finances. It's also important to note that these brackets can change due to annual adjustments for inflation or alterations in tax laws.

Your taxable income is divided into several brackets, each taxed at progressively higher rates. For example, in 2024, the federal income tax rates range from 10% to 37%, with the following brackets for a <u>single</u> filer:

- 10%: $0 to $10,275
- 12%: $10,276 to $41,775
- 22%: $41,776 to $89,075
- 24%: $89,076 to $170,050
- 32%: $170,051 to $215,950
- 35%: $215,951 to $539,900
- 37%: Over $539,900

How does this impact your take-home pay? Understanding your tax bracket is crucial because it directly affects your net income. Higher taxable income may push you into a higher tax bracket, increasing the percentage of your income that goes to taxes. Being aware of your tax bracket can help you make more informed decisions about salary negotiations; job offers and other income opportunities. For example, a higher salary offer might seem attractive on paper, but the additional income could be significantly taxed if it pushes you into a higher bracket. Through education, you can learn strategies to keep your tax liabilities as low as possible.

Tax Deductions and Credits

Tax deductions and credits are crucial tools in reducing your taxable income and consequently, your tax liability. Deductions lower the amount of your income that is subject to tax, while credits reduce your tax bill directly. Together, they can significantly decrease your taxable income, potentially keeping you in a lower tax bracket and saving you money.

Deductions work by reducing your taxable income and may include contributions to retirement accounts, mortgage interest, state and local taxes, and charitable donations. For instance, contributing to a 401(k) or IRA not only helps secure your financial future but also provides immediate tax relief. Mortgage interest deductions can also be substantial for homeowners, while charitable donations offer a double benefit—supporting causes you care about while reducing your tax bill.

Credits, on the other hand, provide a direct reduction in your tax liability. Education credits, such as the American Opportunity Tax Credit and the Lifetime Learning Credit, can significantly offset education expenses. The Child Tax Credit offers financial relief for families with children. Also, credits for energy-efficient home improvements encourage eco-friendly investments while lowering your tax burden.

STRATEGIES FOR TAX PLANNING

Effective tax planning strategies can help you manage your tax bracket and reduce your overall tax burden. Here are some key strategies:

- **Income Splitting**: If possible, distribute income among family members to keep individual incomes in lower tax brackets. For instance, if you own a business, consider hiring your spouse or children. Their wages will be taxed at their lower rate, reducing your overall family tax liability.

- **Deferring Income**: If you anticipate being in a lower tax bracket in the coming years, consider deferring bonuses or other income. For example, if you're expecting a significant year-end bonus, you might request that it be paid in January of the following year instead, shifting the income to a lower-tax period.
- **Maximizing Deductions and Credits**: Strategically plan your charitable contributions, retirement savings, and other deductible expenses throughout the year. For instance, bunching two years' worth of charitable donations into a single tax year can help you exceed the standard deduction and maximize itemized deductions. Similarly, contributing to a Health Savings Account (HSA) provides both immediate tax benefits and long-term health security.
- **Filing Status**: Choosing the most beneficial filing status based on your situation can optimize your tax outcomes. Married couples, for instance, may benefit from filing jointly or separately, depending on their combined income levels and deductions. Filing as "Head of Household" could provide better benefits for single parents than filing as "Single."
- **Retirement Contributions**: Maximizing contributions to tax-advantaged retirement accounts like 401(k)s or IRAs can help reduce your taxable income while securing your future. If you're self-employed, consider a SEP-IRA or Solo 401(k) for even higher contribution limits.
- **Capital Gains Management**: If you have investments, consider managing your capital gains to minimize taxes. For instance, selling losing investments to offset gains (tax-loss harvesting) can help reduce your tax bill. Also, holding investments for more than a year generally qualifies them for lower long-term capital gains rates.

By understanding and effectively utilizing information about tax brackets, deductions, and credits, you can make more informed decisions that optimize your financial situation and reduce your tax liability. Thinking strategically about these things throughout the year can help you make better decisions on the go, not just when it's tax time.

CITY INCOME TAX

The location where you live can significantly impact the amount of taxes you pay, particularly in terms of city income tax rates. City income tax is a tax that some cities impose on income earned by residents within the city limits. Therefore, if you live in a city that has a city income tax, you will be required to pay this tax on top of state and federal income taxes. However, if you live outside the city limits, you will not be required to pay city income tax, which can be a significant advantage. The rates and rules for these taxes can vary significantly. In the United States, forty-two states and many localities impose an income tax on individuals, and the tax rates may be fixed or graduated, varying by state and entity type. Local income taxes are often based on state income tax calculations.

Living outside city limits can have a significant financial advantage as you are not obliged to pay the city's income tax. This means that you can save a considerable amount of money each year on your taxes. As a result, you could save this money, use it for other expenses, or even invest it. By doing so, you can let the returns compound and build towards your retirement savings.

On the other hand, there may be some disadvantages to living outside city limits. You may have to pay higher transportation costs if you need to commute to work or school in the city. Also, you may not have access to the same amenities or services that are available in the city, such as public transportation or cultural events. It will be important to consider this when calculating your potential savings. If you work from home, then this might not apply to you the same way as it would to someone who could be adding time to their commute.

Example of Cincinnati Income Tax:

In the state of Ohio, the city of Cincinnati imposes a city income tax of 1.8% on residents who live within the city limits. If you earn $100,000 per year and live within the city limits, you would be required to pay $1,800 in city income tax. Anyone who lives or works in Cincinnati is subject to this tax regardless of their level of income. This is the rate at the time of writing but could change, so make sure you are researching the current rates for yourself if you are considering moving.

$100,000 X .018 = $1,800 PER YEAR! OR $150 PER MONTH!

However, if you live just outside the city limits in a suburb, you would not be required to pay this tax. That's $1,800 per year that you could keep in your pocket to put to work for you versus handing it over in taxes!

Example of Philadelphia City Income Tax:

Consider Alex, a graphic designer making $50,000 per year. If Alex lived and worked in Philadelphia, under the resident tax rate of approximately 3.8712%, he would owe about $1,935.60 in city income tax. This deduction directly impacts Alex's take-home pay, emphasizing the importance of considering local tax rates in financial planning.

If Alex lives in a nearby suburb like Radnor but commutes to work in Philadelphia, he is subject to the non-resident rate of approximately 3.4481%. With his $50,000 salary, this amounts to about $1,724.05. Although this is slightly less than what he would pay as a resident, it still represents a significant expense.

Individuals living outside the city in places like Radnor or Lower Merion would not owe the city income tax if they did not work in Philadelphia. However, if employed within Philadelphia, the non-resident tax rate applies, impacting their overall net income. This example underscores the importance of understanding local tax laws, which can significantly influence financial decisions, especially when considering employment opportunities and residential locations.

Such local taxes are essential to factor into budgeting, particularly if deciding where to live relative to where you work. It can also be crucial when negotiating salaries or considering a job offer in a different city.

These are just a few great examples of how making a small move can add up to some great savings. Now imagine taking that extra money, investing it, and letting it compound for 30 years. You could supercharge your retirement savings!

SCHOOL DISTRICT INCOME TAXES

One income tax that you may not be able to get away from by simply moving out of the city is school income taxes. Depending on the school district that you are in, there may or may not be an income tax. These tax rates can also vary from district to district. A lot of these taxes are voted on through levies and can change from time to time depending on the results of voting and if levies pass or fail.

School district income taxes can be another factor to consider when deciding where to live. While avoiding them entirely may not be possible, it is worth researching the school district taxes in your area and comparing them to other areas before deciding.

School district income taxes are separate from property taxes and are typically based on a percentage of your income. These taxes are used to fund the local school district and pay for expenses such as teacher salaries, school supplies and building maintenance. Some school districts have a higher income tax rate than others and this can make a significant difference in the amount of money you pay in taxes each year.

One way to save money on school district income taxes is to move to an area that has no school income tax. For example, the state of Texas has no state income tax, but some school districts do impose an income tax. However, there are still many school districts in Texas that do not have an income tax, and moving to one of these areas can save you a significant amount of money each year.

Another location with no school income tax is the state of Nevada. Nevada has no state income tax and no school district income tax, making it an attractive location for individuals looking to save money on taxes. However, property taxes in Nevada can be high, which should be considered when deciding where to live.

When considering the impact of school district income taxes, it is important to look at the long-term effects on your finances. While it may be tempting to move to a location with lower taxes in the short term, it is important to consider the quality of the schools in the area and the potential impact on your children's education. Moving to an area with lower taxes but lower-quality schools may not be the best decision in the long run, as your children's education could be negatively impacted. However, if you can find a location with both low taxes and high-quality schools, it can be a win-

win situation. For example, some areas of Indiana have low school district income taxes and highly rated school systems. By moving to one of these areas, you could save money on taxes while still providing your children with a high-quality education.

When you are considering the tax rates in different school districts, it is also important to consider the potential impact of future levies. As mentioned earlier, school district income taxes can be subject to change based on the results of voting on levies. Suppose you are considering moving to an area with a low-income tax rate. In that case, it is important to research the history of levies in the area and the likelihood of future increases. It is also possible it gets voted down and the tax decreases. However, I would say that it is not very common.

Ultimately, school district income taxes should be another factor to consider when deciding where to live. By researching the tax rates in different areas and considering the long-term impact on your finances, you can make an informed decision about where to live that will benefit both you and your family. While it may not be possible to avoid school district income taxes entirely, moving to an area with lower taxes can help you save money and still provide your children with a high-quality education. If you don't have any children, then the quality of the school district shouldn't matter as much as the money you can save. A little bit of thought and research beforehand can go a long way. That's what we aim for, to provide you with the knowledge so you remember to thoughtfully consider your options. Use this book as a guide towards a clearer path for your future!

COMMUTER TAXES

Commuter taxes, also known as commuter benefit taxes, are taxes imposed by some cities and states on individuals who commute to work from outside of their jurisdiction. These taxes are intended to offset the costs associated with the increased use of local services, such as transportation and infrastructure, by commuters who do not reside in the area. Unfortunately, they try to find every way possible to take more of your hard-earned money.

Commuter taxes are typically levied as a percentage of the individual's income or as a flat fee and can add up to a significant amount of money over time. However, there are ways to avoid paying these taxes.

One option is to move closer to your place of work. By doing so, you may be able to eliminate or reduce the amount of commuter taxes you must pay. This is especially true if you move to an area that does not impose such taxes.

Another option is to explore alternative modes of transportation, such as carpooling, public transportation, or biking. Some cities and states offer tax incentives or credits to individuals who use these modes of transportation, which can help offset the cost of commuter taxes or even eliminate them entirely.

It is important to note that not all cities and states impose commuter taxes. Before making any decisions regarding your commute, it is advisable to research the tax laws in your area to determine whether you will be subject to such taxes. Additionally, you should consult with a tax professional to fully understand your options and any potential tax implications.

One example of a city with a high commuter tax is New York City. Commuters who work in New York City but live outside of the city limits are subject to a commuter tax of up to 3.876%. For someone who earns $100,000 a year, this could result in a tax bill of $3,876. You would need to look at the whole picture to see which direction is best. Moving into town might save you on commuting expenses and make up for any other small tax increases.

$$\$100,000 \times .03876 = \$3,876 \text{ PER YEAR!}$$

Individuals can save thousands of dollars each year by avoiding commuter taxes. It is important to research and understand the tax laws and rates of the areas in which you live and work, to make informed decisions about where to reside and how to manage your finances.

Hopefully, by now you are starting to get the picture of just how much of an impact where you live can have on how much money you get to keep! Moving for money is a great way to keep more hard-earned cash and we are just getting started!

STATE INCOME TAXES

Next up on the list is state income taxes! This can be a big one considering that some states do not have an income tax at all while others can be as high as 13.3% such as in California as it takes the crown for the highest tax rate. If you're looking to save money on your taxes, moving to a state with a more tax-friendly income tax rate can be a smart move. There has been a bit of population migration within the US for this very reason as residents seek out lower taxes and keep more money in their pockets. Some states have progressive tax brackets based on income, and some have fixed tax rates, no matter your income level.

States with the Highest Income Tax Rates:

The states with the highest income tax rates tend to be located on the East and West coasts. According to data from the Tax Foundation, the states with the highest top marginal income tax rates in 2023 were:

1. California: 13.3%
2. Hawaii: 11%
3. New York: 10.9%
4. New Jersey: 10.75%
5. Oregon: 9.9%
6. Minnesota: 9.85%
7. Vermont: 8.75%
8. Iowa: 8.53%
9. Wisconsin: 7.65%
10. Maryland: 5.75%

If you live in one of these states, you may be paying a significant portion of your income in state income taxes. For example, if you make $100,000 per year in California in the top bracket, you would owe $13,030 in state income taxes on that income. That's a substantial amount of money that could be going towards other expenses or savings. I'm just using a round number to illustrate the effect of taxes on the top bracket in the state. Remember, this is just State taxes!

$$\$100,000 \times .133 = \$13,030 \text{ per year in taxes!!}$$

If you make $100,000 total annually in California, you will get into a tax bracket of 9.3% as it is a progressive tax!

Advantages of Moving to a More Tax-Friendly State:

Moving to a state with a more tax-friendly income tax rate can have several advantages. For one, you can keep more of your earnings and potentially save thousands of dollars each year. Additionally, states with lower income tax rates often have lower costs of living, which can allow you to stretch your budget even further.

Another advantage of moving to a more tax-friendly state is that it can open new job opportunities. States with lower income tax rates may be more attractive to businesses, which can lead to increased job growth and economic activity.

States with the Lowest Income Tax Rates:

- Alaska: No state income tax
- Florida: No state income tax
- Nevada: No state income tax
- South Dakota: No state income tax
- Texas: No state income tax
- Washington: No state income tax
- Wyoming: No state income tax
- Tennessee: No state income tax on wages and salaries (but a 1% tax on interest and dividends)
- New Hampshire: There is no state income tax on wages and salaries (but a 5% tax on dividends and interest income). However, depending on these little nuances in the taxes and your situation, it could really add up!
- North Dakota: 1.1% to 2.9%, depending on income level.

If you live in one of these states, you can save a significant amount of money on your taxes each year. For example, if you make

$100,000 per year in Texas, you will owe no state income tax, which means you could potentially save $3,000 or more compared to living in a state with a higher income tax rate.

State income tax rates can significantly impact your finances. If you're looking to save money on your taxes, moving to a state with a more tax-friendly income tax rate can be a smart move. States with no income tax or low-income tax rates can help you keep more of your earnings and potentially save thousands of dollars each year. However, it's essential to consider other factors, such as the cost of living, job opportunities and quality of life, before deciding to move.

Remember to note, that state income tax rates are just one factor to consider when deciding where to live. Other taxes, such as property taxes, sales taxes and business taxes, can also have a significant impact on your finances. Factors such as climate, culture and access to amenities can also play a role in your decision. Before making a move, it's essential to do your research and consider all the factors that are important to you. Remember, you may also want to consult with a financial advisor or tax professional to understand the full impact of state income taxes on your finances.

PROPERTY TAX

Property taxes are a significant expense for homeowners, and they can vary significantly based on where you live. Property taxes are typically rolled into your mortgage payment through escrow when you purchase a home. After your home is paid for, you still owe property tax yearly, that portion of your payment never goes away. Moving to a state or area with lower property tax rates can be intelligent if you are looking to save money on your taxes. We will explore the varying property taxes based on where you live and how you can save money by moving somewhere with lower property tax rates.

Property tax rates vary by state. According to data from the Tax Foundation, the average effective property tax rate in the United States is 1.07%. However, property tax rates can vary significantly, with some states having rates as low as 0.28% and others as high as 2.13%.

States with Low Property Tax Rates:

Hawaii—At 0.28%, Hawaii has the country's lowest average property tax rate, making it an attractive destination for those looking to save money on their property taxes. However, Hawaii is also known for having a high cost of living, so it's essential to consider other factors before deciding to move.

Alabama—Alabama has an average property tax rate of 0.33%, making it one of the most affordable states in terms of property taxes. Alabama also has a lower overall cost of living than many other states, which would be a massive benefit if you're trying to save money.

Colorado - Colorado has an average property tax rate of 0.53%, making it another state with relatively low property taxes. Colorado is known for its natural beauty, outdoor recreation opportunities, and strong economy.

States with High Property Tax Rates:

New Jersey - At 2.13%, New Jersey has the country's highest average property tax rate. This can be a significant expense for homeowners, and it's one reason why many people choose to move out of the state.

Illinois - Illinois has an average property tax rate of 2.05%, making it one of the most expensive states in terms of property taxes. Even after collecting all that tax money, Illinois has struggled with budget deficits and high levels of debt, which can lead to even higher taxes and fees.

Connecticut—Connecticut has an average property tax rate of 1.97%, making it another state with high property taxes. Connecticut also has a higher overall cost of living than many other states, which can be challenging for those on a budget. Combined with its highest income tax rate of 6.99%, Connecticut would be very low on my list of places to live. You would be getting hit from multiple directions in high taxes and high cost of living.

Advantages of Moving:

Moving to a state with lower property tax rates can have several advantages. For one, it can help you save money on your taxes each year. This can allow you to allocate those funds towards other expenses or savings goals and possibly supercharge your retirement fund. Additionally, states with lower property tax rates often have a lower overall cost of living, which can allow you to stretch your budget even further. This can be especially beneficial for retirees or those on a fixed income. It can add up when combined with other tax savings such as low state income tax!

Imagine moving from a state with some of the highest income and property taxes to one of the states with the lowest tax rates! You could cover your mortgage payment with the amount of money you may be able to save.

SALES TAX

After figuring out how to keep as much of your income as possible from where you live, you then also need to figure out the best way to save it when making purchases as well. Sales tax is a tax on the sale of goods and services that is collected by the government at the point of sale. The rate of sales tax can vary depending on where you live, as different states, counties, and cities can set their own rates.

In the United States, the average sales tax rate is around 7%, but rates can range from 0% to as high as 10.5%. Let's look at some examples of the highest and lowest sales tax rates in the US:

Highest Sales Tax Rates:

Tennessee - The state of Tennessee has the highest sales tax rate in the US, with a combined state and local rate of 9.55%.

Louisiana - Louisiana has the second-highest sales tax rate in the US, with a combined state and local rate of 9.52%.

Arkansas - Arkansas has the third-highest sales tax rate in the US, with a combined state and local rate of 9.47%.

Lowest Sales Tax Rates:

Oregon - Oregon is the only state in the US with no sales tax.

Delaware – Delaware has a state sales tax rate of 0%, but some localities impose their own sales taxes.

Montana - Montana has no state sales tax, but some localities do impose their own sales taxes.

When it comes to sales tax, it's important to note that some items, such as food and clothing, may be exempt from sales tax in certain states. Additionally, some states have a lower sales tax rate for necessities like groceries and medicine.

Moving to a state with a lower sales tax rate can be helpful for those looking to save money. For example, if you were to move from Tennessee to Oregon, you would no longer have to pay the high sales tax rate in Tennessee, which could save you a significant amount of money over time. It is important to note from earlier points in the book though, that Tennessee has no state income tax and that could make a bigger impact on savings. It would be best to consider all the taxes when deciding what is most beneficial to your situation and where you are in life. By understanding the sales tax rates in different states, you can make an informed decision when it comes to moving or making large purchases.

BUSINESS INCOME TAXES

Business income tax is a tax on the profits earned by businesses and corporations. The rates for business income tax can vary widely depending on the state where the business is located. Each state sets its rates and determines how it will tax business income.

Highest Business Income Tax Rates

Iowa - Iowa has the highest business income tax rate in the US, with a top rate of 12%.

Pennsylvania - Pennsylvania has the second-highest business income tax rate in the US, with a flat rate of 9.99%.

Minnesota - Minnesota has a top business income tax rate of 9.85%.

Lowest Business Income Tax Rates

Wyoming - Wyoming has no corporate income tax, making it the state with the lowest business income tax rate.

South Dakota - South Dakota also has no corporate income tax.

Nevada - Nevada has a business income tax rate of 1.5%.

The advantages of living in a state with a low business income tax rate can be significant for business owners. By paying less in taxes, business owners can reinvest more money back into their business, which can help to promote growth and expansion. Additionally, states with low business income tax rates may be more attractive to new businesses looking to relocate or expand, which can help to stimulate the economy and create jobs.

On the other hand, states with high business income tax rates may be less attractive to business owners, especially those who are just starting. High taxes can reduce profits, making it more challenging for businesses to survive. Moreover, high taxes can deter new companies from moving to the state, hindering economic growth. It's also important to note that some states offer tax incentives and credits to businesses to encourage economic development. For example, some states offer tax credits for hiring new employees, investing in certain industries, or providing job training programs. By taking advantage of these incentives, businesses can further reduce their tax burden and create a more favorable business environment.

The rates for business income tax can vary significantly by state and business owners need to be aware of these rates and how they can impact their bottom line. By choosing to operate in a state with a lower business income tax rate, business owners can save money and reinvest those savings back into their businesses. When you are a new business trying to make it, this could be the difference between closing up shop or squeezing by in a crunch. Every little bit helps!

Also, it is common for businesses to incorporate in one state but operate in another state or even multiple states. This is because each state has its own laws and regulations regarding business operations, including taxation, liability and reporting requirements. Businesses may choose to incorporate in a state that offers more favorable laws and regulations, such as lower taxes or greater protection from liability, even if they do not operate primarily in that state.

For example, Delaware is a popular state for businesses to incorporate in because of its business-friendly laws and regulations. Delaware has **no sales tax** and **a low corporate income tax rate** and it also offers strong protections for shareholders and directors. As a result, many businesses choose to incorporate in Delaware, even if they do not operate primarily in the state.

However, it's important to note that businesses that operate in multiple states are still subject to the laws and regulations of each state in which they operate. This can be particularly complex when it comes to taxation, as businesses may be subject to different tax laws and rates in each state. In some cases, businesses may need to register to do business in multiple states and comply with various reporting and taxation requirements in each state. Working with a professional is essential to ensure you are meeting all your obligations.

RETIREMENT & TAXES

Retirement! What everyone hopes they can do earlier rather than later and hopefully enjoy for many years. If you are trying to achieve FIRE (Financial Independence, Retire Early), pay close attention! This section and everything up to this point will help get you there.

A primary key to enjoying retirement is ensuring you have enough money to pay the bills and live the life you want. Most people in retirement have passive income from investment dividends and interest and how this income is taxed can vary depending on where you live. Some states tax both dividends and interest income, while others only tax one or the other. Also, states can have different tax rates and exemptions for them.

States Without Tax on Dividends and Interest

States like Alaska, Florida, Nevada, South Dakota, Texas, Washington and Wyoming do not levy a state income tax. Consequently, these regions do not tax dividends and interest income at the state level. This can make them attractive locations for investors seeking to maximize their income from these sources.

States with Uniform Tax Rates for All Income Types

States such as California and New York tax dividends and interest income at the same rates as other types of income. This means that all personal income, regardless of source, is subject to the same taxation rules, simplifying tax planning but may not offer advantages specifically for dividend or interest income.

States with Specific Tax Treatments for Different Income Types

In states like Colorado and Utah, dividends and interest income are taxed at different rates. For example, Colorado offers a lower dividend tax rate than interest income, which can influence investment decisions and tax strategies.

Illinois and Mississippi present another variation where only interest income is taxed, while dividends are exempt. This selective taxation can affect how residents choose to receive their investment incomes.

States Offering Exemptions on Certain Investment Incomes

Connecticut and Rhode Island provide tax exemptions for specific types of interest income, such as that earned from U.S. government bonds. This can make certain investments more favorable under state tax policies.

Kansas and Missouri allow exemptions for a portion of dividend income. Such exemptions can significantly reduce the state tax burden on residents receiving dividend income.

Taxation of Rental Income and The Benefit of Deductions

Many people in retirement use rentals to support their needs. Rental income, like dividends and interest, is subject to taxation but the specific treatment can vary widely depending on the state. Understanding these differences is crucial for real estate investors and landlords as they influence the net income from their rental properties. As stated previously, some states do not impose an income tax period.

Rental income offers several tax benefits that significantly reduce your overall tax liability. Understanding these benefits and how to utilize various deductions is critical for maximizing the profitability of your rental properties.

Deductions

One of the primary deductions available is **depreciation**, which allows you to recover the cost of purchasing and improving a property over its useful life—typically 27.5 years for residential properties and 39 years for commercial ones. The depreciation deduction starts when the property is placed in service and continues annually, lowering your taxable income yearly.

Interest on mortgage loans to buy or improve rental properties is also fully deductible. This includes interest on primary loans and any secondary loans taken out for improvements or other related expenses. This deduction significantly offsets the cost of borrowing by reducing the amount of taxable rental income.

Expenses related to **repairs and maintenance**, including activities like painting, fixing leaks, or replacing broken fixtures, are immediately deductible in the year they are incurred. These expenses must be ordinary, necessary, and reasonable. Additionally, local travel expenses incurred for managing the property, such as mileage for driving to and from the property, are deductible. Suppose you manage rental properties from a home office. In that case, you might qualify to deduct a portion of your home-related expenses, provided the space is used regularly and exclusively for business activities.

Costs for **legal and professional services** related to managing your rental activity, such as fees paid to property management companies, real estate advisors, accountants or attorneys, are fully deductible. These services must directly relate to the operation or management of the rental property.

Insurance premiums for coverage related to your rental activities, including policies for fire, theft, flood damage and landlord liability insurance, are deductible. **Property taxes** paid on the rental property can also be deducted, reducing your taxable income.

These were just a couple of the items to look for in deductions at a high level. If you dive further into it, many different things could be added to this list. Maintaining meticulous records is essential to effectively leveraging these tax deductions. Keep all related receipts, bank statements, mileage logs and other pertinent documentation organized. This will simplify your tax filing process and ensure you are prepared in the event of an IRS audit. By managing these deductions, you can maximize your rental income's profitability, thus enhancing your investment's overall return.

Important Considerations

While some states offer favorable tax treatments for dividends and interest income, it's crucial to remember that these incomes are still subject to federal taxation. The nuances of state tax laws can be complex, so consult with a tax professional to understand the implications and strategize accordingly.

This varied landscape underscores the importance of being aware of your state's specific tax rules, as they can significantly influence your financial planning and investment decisions. Understanding the state-specific tax environment is crucial whether you are investing for growth, income or tax advantages.

When planning for retirement, these are just some things you want to consider and research for the area you are living in or planning to move to. It could mean living on more or less throughout your retirement, and you may even find that after a little research, you could retire earlier than you expected! FIRE!

Financial
Independence
Retire
Early

GENERATING INCOME

> *If you are not willing to risk the unusual, you will have to settle for the ordinary.*

— JIM ROHN

In his quote, Rohn emphasizes the importance of stepping out of your comfort zone and pursuing new opportunities to increase your income. One of the ways you can accomplish this is to buy a property that generates extra income for you. There are many ways to generate income from your property such as leasing land to a farmer, parceling off some lots, renting extra storage space, building an additional unit to rent on a platform such as Airbnb, harvesting timber or even farming or growing plants yourself. Also, I can't forget one of my favorites, house hacking. If you feel stuck and just not meeting your savings goals or need extra cash for bills, maybe moving somewhere new can help you achieve your goals. Also, you may be able to even implement some of these things where you are now.

SHORT TERM RENTALS

Using an extra living space or a separate living area in your home as a short-term rental can be a fantastic way to generate income from your property. I have used short-term rentals for extra income, which has helped us save money and boosted our path to prosperity. Make sure to try to learn everything you can before jumping in.

Utilizing platforms like Airbnb or converting part of your property into an Accessory Dwelling Unit (ADU) can turn your real estate into a profitable source of extra income. Here's how you can maximize the potential of your property through short-term rentals.

Setting Up Your Space for Airbnb

To prepare your space for Airbnb, focus on creating a welcoming and functional environment that will appeal to a broad range of guests. Start by ensuring your rental is clean, well-maintained, and thoughtfully decorated. Invest in quality furnishings and ensure all appliances are in good working order. Take high-quality photos that highlight the best features of your space, such as a cozy reading nook, a spacious kitchen, or a stunning view. Craft a compelling and clear listing description detailing all your property's amenities and unique features. Remember, the goal is to create a space where guests can feel at home.

Understanding Local Regulations

Before listing on Airbnb, it's crucial to understand and comply with the local regulations concerning short-term rentals. This includes zoning laws, permit requirements, safety regulations, and tax obligations. Many cities have specific rules about how many days you can rent your property per year, and some require registering or obtaining a license. Other areas may have homeowner's association (HOA) rules that restrict short-term rentals or building additional units on your property. Check with your local government to ensure you meet all the legal requirements and consider consulting with a legal expert specializing in real estate or short-term rental regulations.

Optimizing Pricing and Bookings

Pricing your rental competitively is key to maximizing occupancy and income—research similar listings in your area to get an idea of market rates. Consider using dynamic pricing tools, such as Price Labs, that automatically adjust your nightly rate based on demand, seasonality, and local events. Keep your calendar up to date and respond quickly to booking inquiries to improve your visibility and attractiveness on the platform. Additionally, offering discounts for longer stays can attract guests looking for extended accommodations, reducing turnover and vacancy rates. AirDNA can be an excellent tool for evaluating your competition and market. Their site will even give you projections on income for a given property.

Providing a Top-Notch Guest Experience

Providing exceptional service can significantly enhance guest satisfaction, lead to positive reviews, and repeat bookings. Offer an individualized touch, such as a welcome note, a small gift, or local treats. Provide essential items such as toiletries, fresh linens and basic kitchen supplies to make your guests' stay more comfortable. Ensure a straightforward check-in process and be available to answer any questions or resolve issues promptly. Solicit feedback from your guests to improve their experience and your listing.

Location

Your property's location can also impact its potential as a short-term rental or for building an additional unit. You'll want to consider the proximity to local attractions, public transportation, and other amenities that may be attractive to potential renters.

Property Features

When evaluating a property for its potential as a short-term rental, you'll want to consider its size, layout, and amenities. Does it have enough space for multiple guests? Is there a private entrance for the rental unit? Are there amenities that guests may find attractive, such as a pool or outdoor space? Doing a little research, you can see what amenities provide the highest return in the area you want to establish.

Property condition

The property's condition is also important to consider, as it will impact the amount of work and money you may need to put into it before it's ready for renters. You'll want to evaluate the property's overall condition, including the roof, plumbing, electrical and HVAC systems. You will want to make it as lovely as possible to stand out from similar properties.

Rental income potential

Finally, you'll want to evaluate the property's potential rental income. Research the local rental market to get an idea of what you could charge for a short-term rental or additional unit and compare this to the costs associated with purchasing or renovating the property. Again, an excellent site for checking out your rental potential is AirDNA. You can find out how they rate your area for short-term rentals and even see what revenue other people are pulling in.

Some areas may be more favorable for short-term rentals than others. Popular tourist destinations may have a higher demand for short-term rentals, which could translate into higher rental income potential. In other areas, such as suburban or rural areas, there may not be as much demand for short-term rentals, which would translate to fewer bookings and income.

One nice thing you can do with Airbnb is rent out an extra room or a living area in the basement with its own entrance. You don't have to rent them out every night to make a decent amount of extra income. If you make the space clean and comfortable for your guests and take some good pictures for the booking site, you should continue to get some bookings. Make sure to communicate well and ask for reviews. Having multiple 5-star reviews will help increase your bookings.

Example of Utilizing Unused Space for Income

Imagine you own a property with a garage that features a finished living space above it. Enhancing this space with a bathroom and a small kitchenette could transform it into a cozy rental unit suitable for Airbnb guests. Let's say you set the rental price at $70 per night. Even without the advantage of being located in a tourist hotspot, it's reasonable to expect that you could fill the space for a few nights each month.

Suppose you rent out the unit for an average of 5 nights each month. This arrangement would generate an additional $350 per month. This extra income could help cover monthly expenses or save for future financial goals. Moreover, the addition of functional living space not only generates immediate income but also potentially increases the overall value of your property. Adding amenities that improve the livability of any space typically enhances its appeal to future buyers, thereby driving up property value.

Should you ever decide to sell your property, these upgrades and the potential for rental income can make your home more attractive to prospective buyers, potentially increasing your return on investment. This strategic use of space provides immediate financial benefits and contributes to long-term financial security.

To Sum It Up: By carefully preparing your space, understanding and adhering to local laws, optimizing your pricing strategy, and focusing on guest experience, you can successfully generate significant extra income through Airbnb and ADUs. These efforts boost your rental's appeal and enhance your reputation as a host, paving the way for a successful short-term rental venture.

If you are contemplating moving, these are some things you may want to keep in mind when choosing a home. Picking a property that can potentially create rentable space quickly can help you generate extra cash. When considering a move for this purpose, it's important to research and evaluate the potential risks and rewards. Consider working with a real estate professional with experience in this area to help you make the best-informed decisions.

RENTING SPACE OR STORAGE

Exploring opportunities to monetize unused spaces in your home can transform dormant areas into profitable ventures. Various platforms offer user-friendly solutions for renting out different types of space, whether for storage, events, or leisure. Peer Space, Neighbor, and Swimply are just a few examples of apps that facilitate these rentals.

Peer Space specializes in hourly rentals for diverse needs such as meetings, photo shoots, or small gatherings. This flexibility allows property owners to use their vacant studios or rooms without committing to long-term agreements. **Neighbor** provides a platform for homeowners to rent out unused storage space, connecting them with people needing storage solutions nearby. **Swimply** allows property owners to rent out private pools by the hour, which can be a compelling reason to invest in a property with a pool, providing both a luxury for the family and a potential income stream.

Before diving into the rental market, it's crucial to understand the local regulations and logistical considerations involved:

- **Local Zoning Regulations:** Begin by consulting local zoning laws to ensure your plans for renting out space are permissible. Some residential areas may have restrictions on the type of commercial activities allowed.
- **Property Insurance:** Review your insurance policy to confirm that it covers liabilities associated with renting out your space. It is advisable to require tenants to have their own renter's insurance to cover their possessions, further mitigating your risk.
- **Lease Agreement:** A clear, written lease agreement should outline all terms of the rental arrangement, including payment terms, duration and conditions for space usage. Ensure it addresses access rules, maintenance responsibilities and security measures.
- **Tenant Screening:** Conduct thorough screenings for potential tenants, including credit and background checks. This step is vital to ensure reliability and timely payments.
- **Security:** Implement appropriate security measures to protect the rented space and tenants' belongings. This might include installing quality locks and surveillance cameras and setting access limitations.
- **Taxes:** Be aware of local tax requirements that may apply to rental income. Some regions require landlords to collect sales tax on the revenue generated from renting out space.

Renting out unused space can be a lucrative strategy for generating additional income, but it's essential to approach this venture with a well-informed, strategic plan. You can effectively and safely capitalize on your property's potential by understanding and adhering to local regulations, ensuring proper legal and insurance safeguards and maintaining high security and tenant management standards.

LEASING LAND

For those residing in rural areas with ample unused acreage, leasing land presents a viable opportunity to generate income and optimize land use. Whether your land is suited for farming or nestled in a region ideal for hunting, understanding how to leverage these assets can lead to financial benefits while contributing to agricultural and recreational activities.

Leasing Land for Farming If your property is in a region conducive to agriculture, partnering with a farmer could be advantageous. This arrangement not only generates steady income but also ensures that your land remains productive and well-maintained. Here are key considerations for leasing land for farming:

- **Types of Lease Agreements**: Choosing the appropriate lease agreement that aligns with your financial goals and risk tolerance is crucial. A cash rent lease, where the farmer pays a fixed amount annually, offers predictability and ease of management. Alternatively, a crop share lease, where you receive a portion of the crop yield, potentially increases profitability but involves more risk and requires closer involvement in farm operations.
- **Understanding the Farmer's Needs**: It is essential to collaborate with the farmer to understand their operational requirements. This might include discussions on organic farming practices, which may dictate the use of certain chemicals and fertilizers, as well as infrastructure needs like irrigation and fencing.
- **Setting Clear Expectations**: Establish clear terms for the lease, such as its duration, rent specifics, and usage restrictions. Ensure all agreements are documented in writing to prevent future disputes.

- **Consider Liability Issues**: Address potential liabilities by ensuring adequate safety measures are in place and requiring the farmer to carry liability insurance. This protects both you and the lessee from unexpected legal or financial burdens.
- **Plan for the Long-term**: Consider farming practices' sustainability and environmental impact. Planning for soil fertility and crop rotation can help maintain the land's productivity for future use.

Leasing Land for Hunting Leasing land for hunting can be particularly lucrative in areas known for wildlife, such as regions with abundant deer populations. Hunters often seek exclusive access to private lands, which can command premium lease rates.

- **Understand Local Demand**: Gauge interest and pricing in your area by researching what local hunters are looking for and what other landowners are charging.
- **Set Terms and Conditions**: Clearly define what is allowed under the lease, such as the types of game that can be hunted, the hunting methods permitted, and the seasons when hunting is allowed. This helps manage the hunter's expectations and ensures compliance with local wildlife regulations.
- **Safety and Liability**: Ensure your land is safe for hunting activities and consider the liability implications. Requiring hunters to carry their own insurance can mitigate potential risks.
- **Promote Conservation**: If conservation is a priority, you can include terms that promote sustainable hunting practices to ensure wildlife populations are not adversely impacted.

Leasing your land for farming or hunting not only provides a financial return but also helps in the stewardship of your land, supporting local food production or wildlife management. You can create enduring and profitable leasing arrangements by carefully considering your options and establishing clear, mutually beneficial agreements.

HARVESTING TIMBER

Another way to generate income from a potential property is through forest management and timber sales. There are many things to consider when doing this, but it can be very successful.

I have used this opportunity to decide to buy a property and determine if it was the right deal for me. I was not only moving to take advantage of better tax rates, but I was also looking for ways to generate income from the property I was interested in to get an even better deal. I was able to use the money from the select cut on the property's timber to pay for remodeling the entire inside of the house! Then considering the thousands of dollars a year I was saving in taxes and utilities I was able to pay off debts and start saving at much higher rates as well. To go even further, when I moved again, I turned this house into a short-term rental. It generated six figures in revenue in the first year! Talk about a winner! This property was a great example of how using the strategies in this book can supercharge your finances.

When looking to generate some cash through selling timber here are some things to consider:

- **Understand the Value of Your Timber**: Before selling timber, it's important to know the value of the trees you have on your property. Many factors determine the value of timber, such as species, size, quality, and market demand. Consulting with a professional forester can help you understand the value of your timber and make informed decisions about selling it.

- **Develop a Management Plan**: Sustainable forest management is essential to maintaining healthy forests and ensuring the long-term viability of your timber. A professional forester can help you develop a management plan that considers factors such as tree growth rates, soil conditions and wildlife habitat needs. The plan should outline how you will harvest trees and replant them to ensure the continued health of your forest.

- **Choose a Reputable Buyer**: When selling timber, it's important to choose a reputable buyer who values sustainable forest management. Look for buyers who are certified by organizations such as the Forest Stewardship Council (FSC) or the Sustainable Forestry Initiative (SFI). These organizations ensure that buyers are following sustainable practices and support the responsible management of forests.

- **Harvest Timber Responsibly**: Once you've identified a buyer and developed a management plan, it's important to harvest your timber responsibly. This means using sustainable harvesting techniques such as selective cutting, which allows some trees to remain standing to provide habitat for wildlife and maintain the health of the forest. Avoid clear-cutting, which can have negative impacts on soil erosion, water quality and wildlife habitat. Not to mention, it leaves the land looking demolished and unpleasant.

- **Replant Trees**: After harvesting timber, it's important to replant trees to maintain the health of the forest and ensure a sustainable timber supply for future generations. Replanting should consider factors such as soil conditions, tree species and wildlife habitat needs. A professional forester can help you develop a replanting plan that meets these criteria. In my personal experience, I did not need to replant trees because the forest was already thick and we only took select trees.

Selling timber from your property can generate income and have other benefits. For example, it can help maintain the health and biodiversity of your forest, provide habitat for wildlife, and reduce the risk of forest fires by removing dead or diseased trees.

Overall, selling timber from your property can be a smart financial decision, but it's important to approach it with a focus on sustainable forest management to ensure the long-term health of your forest and the viability of your timber supply.

DEVELOPMENT

This can be a big one! Land development represents a significant opportunity for property owners to maximize their investment and potentially yield substantial returns. Whether you're considering purchasing a new property or optimizing the value of the land you own, incorporating development into your strategy is wise. Here's how to approach land development thoughtfully and effectively.

Conducting a Feasibility Study

Assessing your investment's viability and potential returns is crucial before you begin any development project. A comprehensive feasibility study will help you understand the economic dynamics at play. This study should evaluate market demand, zoning regulations, environmental constraints, and infrastructure requirements. Understanding these factors will inform your decisions and shape your development strategy.

Subdividing the Land

Subdividing your land into smaller parcels is a standard method for increasing its overall value. This process involves partitioning the land into distinct sections, which can be sold individually, often at a premium. However, subdivision requires meticulous planning and adherence to local regulations. You'll need to obtain the necessary approvals from local authorities, conduct accurate surveying and install essential utilities like water, sewer and electricity. Each step ensures that the subdivided parcels are viable for sale or further development.

Developing the Land

Turning raw land into developed property for residential or commercial use can significantly enhance its market value. Whether you're building homes, commercial complexes, or mixed-use developments, each project should align with market needs and local planning regulations. Engage with urban planners and construction experts to ensure your development projects are well-designed and fulfill all legal requirements.

Enhancing the Land

Improving the land's natural features and accessibility can also increase its attractiveness and value. Consider implementing enhancements such as clearing overgrown areas, landscaping, and adding recreational amenities like parks, trails, or lakes. These improvements make the property more appealing to potential buyers or renters and contribute to the community's well-being, making the investment more desirable.

Strategic Considerations

When exploring options for land development, always consider long-term implications and sustainability. Developments should enhance the land without degrading its natural resources or beauty. Strategic planning, in collaboration with environmental consultants and local stakeholders, will help ensure your development projects are profitable and environmentally responsible.

Land development can be an effective way to generate significant income and increase the value of your property by carefully planning and executing these strategies. This approach not only offers financial benefits but can also lead to the creation of thriving new communities and valuable real estate assets.

HOUSE HACKING

This is one of my favorite ways for people to get into real estate and make some extra money from a property. House hacking could potentially cover your entire mortgage. I believe anyone looking to purchase their first property should consider this one of their top options, as should anyone just trying to reduce their living expenses.

What is house hacking? House hacking is a strategic real estate investment approach where you use your primary residence to generate income, significantly reducing or even eliminating your housing costs. This method not only eases your financial burden but can also introduce you to the basics of real estate investing. Here's how to successfully navigate the process of house hacking.

Leveraging Your Primary Residence

The core idea behind house hacking is to make your primary residence work for you. This could involve buying a multi-unit property and living in one unit while renting out the others or renting out a basement or separate floor of a single-family home. The rental income generated from these additional units can cover your mortgage, taxes, and possibly other living expenses, effectively allowing you to live for free or at a significantly reduced cost.

Finding the Right Property

Identifying the ideal property for house hacking involves several key considerations:

- **Location**: Look for properties in desirable areas that attract renters, such as near schools, public transportation, and amenities.
- **Layout**: The property's layout should ideally provide privacy and separate living spaces for you and your tenants. Duplexes, triplexes, or homes with finished basements or above-garage apartments are particularly well-suited for this strategy.
- **Financing Options**: Consider the financing requirements for multi-family properties, which may differ from those for single-family homes. Research available loan options that cater specifically to potential house hackers.

Navigating the Mortgage Process

Securing a mortgage for a house-hack property can be unique:

- **Loan Types**: Residential mortgages for multi-unit properties (up to four units) are available, but you must inform the lender of your intention to rent out part of the property. FHA loans can be especially advantageous for first-time house hackers due to lower down payment requirements and the allowance of up to four units.
- **Lender Considerations**: Lenders will consider the potential rental income from the property when assessing your loan application, which can help you qualify for a larger loan. However, they will also scrutinize your landlord's capabilities and any property management experience you might have.

Managing Tenants and Leases

Being a landlord is an integral part of house hacking and requires careful management:

- **Screening Tenants**: Implement a thorough screening process, including credit checks, employment verification, and references. This helps ensure you find reliable tenants who will pay rent on time and maintain the property.
- **Lease Agreements**: Draft clear and comprehensive lease agreements that outline the terms and conditions of the rental, including the rent amount, payment deadlines, and maintenance responsibilities. Adhere to local landlord-tenant laws and regulations.
- **Tenant Management**: Develop good communication and management practices to maintain positive tenant

relationships. Address maintenance issues promptly and enforce lease terms fairly and respectfully.

House hacking offers a practical entry into real estate investment and can significantly offset or eliminate personal living expenses. By carefully selecting the right property, securing appropriate financing, and effectively managing tenants, you can enjoy the dual benefits of free living and valuable investment experience.

Let's check out an example to see how this could work for you.

Consider the case of Sarah, a first-time homebuyer and aspiring real estate investor in Denver, Colorado. Sarah purchased a duplex for $400,000 and intended to live in one unit and rent out the other.

Purchase and Financing Details:

- **Property Price:** $400,000
- **Down Payment:** 5% (FHA Loan) = $20,000
- **Loan Amount:** $380,000
- **Interest Rate:** 3.5%
- **Mortgage Payment (including principal and interest):** Approximately $1,706 per month
- **Property Taxes and Insurance:** Approximately $450 per month
- **Total Monthly Mortgage Expense:** $2,156

Rental Income:

- Sarah decides to live in one unit of the duplex and rent out the other. The going rate for similar units in her area is $1,500 monthly.
- **Monthly Rental Income:** $1,500

Operating Expenses:

- **Utilities (water, sewer, garbage):** Sarah pays $200 monthly and splits the costs with her tenant.
- **Maintenance and Repairs:** Budgeted at $100 monthly to cover minor repairs and maintenance issues.

Net Operating Income Calculation:

- **Total Monthly Income:** $1,500 (rental income)
- **Total Monthly Expenses:** $2,456 ($2,156 mortgage + $200 utilities + $100 maintenance)
- **Monthly Cash Outflow:** $956 ($2,456 - $1,500)

Analysis: While Sarah has a monthly cash outflow of $956, she is effectively living in her home for less than half the typical cost for a similar property in her area. Typically, renting a comparable unit would cost around $1,500 per month, which means she saves $544 monthly. Additionally, Sarah benefits from building equity in the property as her tenants help pay down the mortgage.

Long-Term Financial Impact:

- As the mortgage principal is paid down and property values potentially increase, Sarah's equity in the property grows.
- She can eventually decide to move out and rent both units, potentially doubling her rental income to $3,000 per month. If the mortgage and operating costs remain constant, her cash flow could turn positive, creating a profitable investment.

This real-life scenario illustrates how house hacking can significantly reduce living expenses while providing a pathway to real estate investment. Despite the initial monthly outflow, Sarah effectively reduces her living expenses and positions herself for future financial gains. Over time, her investment could shift from being cost-saving to income-generating, especially if rental rates increase or she decides to leverage equity to expand her investment portfolio. When Sarah goes to move, if she continues to implement the strategies in this book and the plan of Moving for money, she will find herself on a path toward financial freedom and prosperity.

Whether you're house hacking to cover your mortgage, developing land to enhance its value, or utilizing spaces like garages or basements for short-term rentals on platforms like Airbnb, the key to success lies in meticulous planning and strategic execution. Understanding local regulations, optimizing property features, and ensuring your ventures are legally sound and financially feasible are crucial steps that can lead to significant financial benefits.

As we wrap up this chapter, remember that these strategies aim to generate income and build long-term wealth. By carefully considering each opportunity and its implications, you can create a robust financial foundation supporting your current needs and future ambitions.

Reflect and Apply:

1. **Considering Your Property**: Think about your current living situation. Do you have any unused space or property that could be converted into a short-term rental, storage space, or leased for farming or other uses? What steps

could you take to start generating income from these opportunities?

2. **Exploring New Income Streams**: Which income-generating strategies discussed in this chapter (short-term rentals, leasing land, timber harvesting, house hacking, development) resonate most with you? Why? What first steps can you take to explore and implement this strategy?

By reflecting on these questions, you can start to identify actionable steps to enhance your financial situation using the strategies discussed in Chapter 3. Remember, the journey to financial empowerment begins with small, deliberate actions.

GETTING PAID TO MOVE, MOVING FOR MONEY

> *Your life does not get better by chance, it gets better by change.*
>
> — JIM ROHN

Relocating for a job or asking to relocate can be both an exciting opportunity and a significant financial undertaking. Understanding and negotiating employer relocation packages can significantly ease the transition by covering moving costs and setting up in a new location. Here's what you need to know about employer relocation packages and how to ensure you get the best possible deal.

UNDERSTANDING EMPLOYER RELOCATION PACKAGES

Employer relocation packages are typically designed to financially support employees who are moving for work-related reasons. These packages can vary widely depending on the company, the role, and the distance of the move. Typically, they may cover:

- **Moving Expenses:** This can include packing, transporting, and unpacking your belongings.
- **Travel Costs:** Expenses for traveling to the new location, such as airfare or gas, possibly including family members.
- **Temporary Housing:** Some employers offer temporary housing or a stipend for the first few months as you settle into the new area.
- **Job Search Assistance for Spouse:** Some companies offer job search support if relocating also affects a spouse's or partner's employment.
- **Miscellaneous Expenses:** These might include storage fees, visa and immigration assistance, and other incidentals.

What to Look for in a Relocation Package

When evaluating a relocation package, consider the comprehensive coverage of all potential costs and any possible gaps that might leave you out of pocket. Here are vital aspects to look for:

- **Comprehensiveness:** Does the package cover all the major expenses related to the move, or will you need to pay out of pocket for significant items?
- **Flexibility:** Does the package offer a lump sum or reimbursement for actual expenses? A lump sum might provide more flexibility but requires careful budgeting to ensure all costs are covered.
- **Support Services:** Beyond covering costs, some packages include support services such as help finding schools or real estate agents, which can be invaluable in unfamiliar surroundings.
- **Tax Implications:** Understand who is responsible for any tax liabilities associated with relocation benefits, as some benefits may be taxable.

Negotiating a Relocation Package

If the initial relocation package offered doesn't fully meet your needs, remember that these packages are often negotiable. Here's how to approach negotiations:

- **Assess Your Needs:** Before entering negotiations, clearly understand your needs and which elements of the package are most important to you.
- **Do Your Research:** Understand typical relocation assistance for your industry and role to help frame your expectations and negotiations.
- **Be Clear and Professional:** When discussing the package with your employer, clarify what you need, why it's necessary, and how it will help facilitate a smoother transition.

- **Highlight Your Value:** Remind your employer of the value you bring to the company and how the relocation contributes to your ability to perform effectively.

Successfully negotiating a relocation package that adequately covers your needs can significantly improve your moving experience and ensure that you start in your new location on the right foot. Whether moving across the country or to a different nearby city, a well-rounded package can alleviate financial stress, allowing you to focus on excelling in your new position or home.

CITIES THAT WILL PAY YOU TO MOVE THERE

In an effort to stimulate local economies and attract talent, several cities and states across the country have introduced incentive programs designed to entice new residents. These initiatives often include cash incentives, tax breaks and other benefits. This creates unique opportunities for those looking to relocate. This section explores various programs, discusses eligibility requirements, shares success stories and provides considerations for those considering a move.

Incentive Programs and Opportunities Across the US

In recent years, many cities and states have recognized the benefits of attracting new talent and crafted incentive programs to draw individuals and families from other regions. These programs often extend beyond simple cash offers, providing a comprehensive package designed to ease the transition and integrate new residents into the community. Here's a more detailed look at various programs across the United States, each offering unique benefits to prospective movers.

Tulsa, Oklahoma - Tulsa Remote One of the most publicized programs is Tulsa Remote, which offers $10,000 to remote workers who move to Tulsa and stay for at least one year. Participants receive membership to a coworking space and assistance in integrating into the community through organized events and activities.

Topeka, Kansas—Choose Topeka The city's program, Choose Topeka, offers up to $15,000 for individuals moving to work onsite in the area and $10,000 for remote workers relocating there. This initiative is part of a broader strategy to boost the local economy by attracting diverse professionals.

Savannah, Georgia—Savannah Technology Workforce Incentive This program targets technology workers and offers up to $2,000 in moving costs for qualified tech professionals who relocate to Savannah. The goal is to bolster the city's growing tech sector by attracting skilled talent.

Hamilton, Ohio - Talent Attraction Program Scholarship Hamilton offers a reverse scholarship program that pays up to $10,000 to recent college graduates who move to the city. This initiative aims to attract young professionals who can contribute to the local economy and community life.

Northwest Arkansas - Life Works Here The Life Works Here initiative by the Northwest Arkansas Council offers $10,000 and provides a bicycle to remote workers who move to the region. The incentive is designed to draw in professionals who can work from anywhere but are seeking a high quality of life, which the scenic and vibrant Northwest Arkansas region offers.

Vermont - Remote Worker Grant Program Vermont's program provides reimbursements up to $7,500 over two years to cover moving expenses, computer software and hardware, broadband access and coworking memberships. This is part of Vermont's broader strategy to counteract its aging population by attracting younger remote workers.

Eligibility Requirements While these programs are attractive, they come with specific eligibility requirements to ensure the benefits are mutually advantageous. Typical criteria include maintaining full-time employment, residing in the area for a set period, or participating in community activities. Some programs may require applicants to work in specific sectors or demonstrate a certain income level to ensure that new residents contribute economically to the community.

Success Stories The impact of these incentive programs can be profound, both for the individuals and the communities they join. These stories highlight the potential for such programs to not only change lives but also rejuvenate communities.

1. Moving to Tulsa, Oklahoma Benjamin's Story: Benjamin was a freelance graphic designer living in a high-cost city on the West Coast. He discovered the Tulsa Remote program, which offered $10,000 and additional benefits such as a coworking space membership to remote workers willing to relocate to Tulsa. Facing the increasing cost of living and looking for a change of scenery, Benjamin decided to apply to the program.

Upon acceptance, he relocated to Tulsa. The incentive helped him cover all moving expenses and settle in without financial strain. The coworking space provided through the program allowed him to network with other professionals and integrate into the local community. Not only did the move dramatically reduce his living expenses, but the networking opportunities also led to new clients and a significant expansion of his freelance business. Benjamin's story highlights how such a move can lower living costs and enhance professional growth.

2. Moving to Topeka, Kansas Emily's Story: Emily was a recent college graduate from the University of Michigan, working in an underwhelming job that didn't utilize her degree in business administration. She learned about the Choose Topeka program, which offers up to $15,000 to individuals who relocate to Topeka and work locally. Intrigued by the possibility of a fresh start and financial support, Emily applied for a job in Topeka, got hired and moved.

The relocation package helped Emily afford a down payment on a small home, a feat that would have been nearly impossible in her previous city due to high real estate prices. The financial relief allowed her to focus on her new job and personal development. In Topeka, Emily found not only a fulfilling career path but also engaged in community activities that enriched her social life. Her move to Topeka illustrates how relocation incentives can offer both professional and personal rejuvenation.

These stories exemplify the transformative potential of relocation incentive programs. Both individuals leveraged these programs' financial and supportive aspects to significantly improve their quality of life, accelerate their careers, and achieve unattainable personal goals in their previous locations.

Considerations Before Moving

While the financial incentives are appealing, it's crucial to consider other factors before deciding to relocate:

- **Cost of Living**: Evaluate how the cost of living in the new area compares to your current location. Lower housing costs can significantly increase your quality of life, but other expenses may be higher.

- **Employment Opportunities**: Ensure there are sufficient job opportunities in your field unless you're moving specifically for a remote work arrangement.
- **Lifestyle Changes**: Consider the area's cultural and social aspects. The pace of life, community values and local amenities should align with your lifestyle preferences and long-term goals.

Before making a decision, it's advisable to visit the area, speak with locals, and realistically assess whether the move aligns with your personal and professional objectives. Ultimately, these incentive programs offer more than just financial benefits; they offer a chance to reshape your life in a new setting with new opportunities and challenges.

UTILITY CONSIDERATIONS

When relocating, whether for a job opportunity or to take advantage of an incentive program, understanding the types and costs of utilities in your new location is essential. This knowledge can help you budget effectively and even save money. This section explores the various utilities you might encounter, strategies for reducing utility bills, and differences in utility options between rural and urban settings. Additionally, we'll investigate sustainable options that can further enhance your home's efficiency and environmental friendliness.

Utilities encompass a wide range of crucial services for comfortable and functional home life. These include:

- **Gas and Propane**: Used primarily for heating and cooking. Costs can vary significantly depending on local suppliers and market rates.

- **Electric**: Powers lighting, appliances, and electronic devices. Rates can fluctuate based on usage and time of day in some areas.
- **Water**: Essential for daily living, water costs can vary depending on municipal water sources versus private water systems.
- **Stormwater Management**: Often billed separately in cities to handle runoff and prevent flooding.
- **Cable, Internet, Satellite, and Fiber**: Entertainment and connectivity services, with prices influenced by the level of service and competition in the area.
- **Trash and Recycling Services**: Typically managed by the municipality or contracted out to private companies, with fees based on service levels.

You will encounter These main types of utilities when looking for a place to live.

Going Green

Adopting green utilities not only helps the environment but can also lead to significant savings. Some other green options to consider are:

- **Solar Panels**: Installing solar panels can drastically reduce your electricity bills and may qualify you for tax incentives.
- **Geothermal Systems**: Although expensive to install, geothermal heating and cooling systems offer long-term savings and environmental benefits.
- **Rainwater Harvesting**: Collecting and using rainwater for gardening and other non-potable water use can reduce municipal water usage.

By understanding the types of utilities available, employing strategies to reduce usage, and considering sustainable options, you can manage your utility costs more effectively and contribute to a healthier environment. Whether moving to a bustling city or a serene rural area, these green considerations will help you make informed decisions that suit your lifestyle and budget.

Saving Money on Utilities

Reducing utility expenses is an essential aspect of managing household budgets effectively. Here are some strategies and practical tips to help minimize utility costs, enhance energy efficiency and make the most of your utility services:

1. Conduct a Home Energy Audit

Start with a professional home energy audit. This assessment can pinpoint where your home is losing energy and what steps you can take to improve efficiency. Auditors use tools like blower doors and infrared cameras to detect air leaks and insulation gaps. Based on the audit results, you can prioritize the most cost-effective improvements.

2. Upgrade to Energy-Efficient Appliances

Old appliances not only consume more energy but can also add unnecessary costs to your utility bills. When upgrading your refrigerator, dishwasher, washing machine and dryer, look for ENERGY STAR-certified appliances. These appliances meet strict energy efficiency guidelines set by the U.S. Environmental Protection Agency and can save you money in the long run.

3. Install Smart Thermostats

Smart thermostats allow for more precise control over your home heating and cooling, which can significantly reduce energy consumption. These devices learn your schedule and temperature preferences to optimize your home's HVAC system. You can also control them remotely via smartphone, making it easy to adjust settings when you're away from home, ensuring you're not heating or cooling an empty house.

4. Implement Water-Saving Measures

Water bills can be reduced by installing water-efficient fixtures. Low-flow showerheads, toilets and faucet aerators can dramatically decrease water usage. Additionally, promptly fixing leaks is crucial— a small drip can waste a substantial amount of water over time.

5. Enhance Home Insulation

Proper insulation helps retain heat during winter and keeps your home cool in the summer, reducing the need for constant heating and cooling. Check attics, basements, and crawl spaces and add insulation where necessary. Sealing gaps around doors and windows with weather stripping or caulk can also prevent energy loss.

6. Switch to LED Lighting

LED bulbs use at least 75% less energy and last 25 times longer than traditional incandescent lighting. Switching all your home's lighting to LED can lower the portion of your electricity bill related to lighting. Consider automating lighting with timers or smart systems to reduce usage further.

7. Optimize Your Water Heater Settings

Water heating is a significant part of energy consumption. Lowering the water heater thermostat to 120 degrees Fahrenheit can reduce power usage without sacrificing comfort. Additionally, insulating your water heater and the first few feet of hot and cold water pipes can prevent heat loss.

8. Use Power Strips and Unplug Electronics

Many appliances and electronic devices draw power even when turned off, a phenomenon known as "phantom load." Using power strips to turn off televisions, stereos, and computers can eliminate this hidden energy use. Unplugging chargers when not in use is another simple way to save.

By integrating these strategies, you can achieve considerable savings on your utilities. Each step reduces your monthly bills and supports a more sustainable lifestyle. Look around your home; what things can you do now to start saving?

Rural Versus Urban

When deciding between rural and urban living, understanding the differences in utility access and costs is crucial, as these factors significantly influence overall expenses. You won't get a monthly bill for some utilities living in an urban area, but there can be some high upfront costs if you build a home. Also, some maintenance items may be needed if you buy an existing home with systems already in place.

Water Supply and Sewage Systems

Typically, **urban** residents have access to municipal (City) water and sewer systems. These systems are generally reliable and require little maintenance from the homeowner, but the cost is often higher due to higher infrastructure and service costs in densely populated areas. City dwellers usually pay monthly fees based on usage, which can add up, especially in households with high water usage. These bills never seem to get any smaller, and like all city utilities, they seem to have only gotten more expensive over recent years.

Rural homes often rely on wells for water and septic systems for sewage disposal. Initially, installing a well or septic system can be a significant expense, but operational costs tend to be lower than municipal services. However, maintenance is crucial; failing to maintain a septic system properly or well can lead to costly repairs. Well water may also require additional filtration or treatment systems depending on the water quality, which can add to the expense. If you're buying an existing home, inspecting these systems and ensuring they are functioning correctly is essential. Also, in most areas, you can find a water company that will test your water quality for free and suggest any additional treatment equipment needed.

Questions to ask and what to look for when buying a home in a rural area:

1. How deep is the well? A deep well could mean more cost if you have to work on it in the future or drill a new one.
2. How well does the well perform? You can turn on the hose for some water wells and let it run for hours without issues. For other wells, you may be limited and they could run dry upon heavy usage.
3. How old is water treatment equipment such as a water softener? I currently have one in one of my properties and it is going on eight years old with no issues. You may have to spend maybe $15 monthly to buy the salt. The unit costs about $500 upfront and should last many years. Keep in mind that you have no monthly water bill like in the city!
4. When was the last time the septic tank was pumped? If the septic system includes a holding tank, it should be pumped every couple of years to maintain its longevity.

5. If the septic system's location is not apparent, ask if they have a drawing of the leach field and if the system was permitted when installed.

I prefer the utilities of the country. If you know what to look for and have quality systems, you can eliminate the monthly water and sewage bill you get nailed with living in the city and have even higher-quality water. There is no chlorine, fluoride, or other additives they might be using to treat the water. If you live somewhere like Flint, Michigan, then I'm sure anything else would be better!

Energy Supply

Urban settings usually provide easy access to various energy sources, such as natural gas, electricity, and in some cases, district heating systems. The infrastructure is well-established, offering a stable and continuous energy supply. However, urban consumers may face higher energy rates due to greater demand and higher delivery costs. These rates have been rocketing higher and rarely pull back once they get them raised.

Rural energy options can be more limited. Many rural homes rely on propane or fuel oil for heating, which can be more expensive and require pre-planning to ensure adequate supplies throughout the heating season. Electricity is available but rural areas are more susceptible to power outages due to fewer redundancies in the grid and greater exposure to the elements affecting infrastructure. On the positive side, rural areas offer more opportunities for sustainable energy solutions like solar panels or wind turbines due to more available space and fewer regulatory hurdles. Installing a generator is one way to eliminate the risk of a power outage during a weather event. These can run from natural gas, propane, gas or diesel. Also, you can get a smaller portable generator to have on standby and have an electrician put in the necessary plugs and wiring to make it a quick hook-up when needed.

Some questions you can ask about energy utilities when looking to buy a rural home:

1. Is there a whole home generator? If not, you may consider budgeting for one in the future. In my experience, power outages are few and far between and last only a couple of hours. We have a portable generator that can be hooked up at the meter in an outage and power the necessities in the home.

2. What is the heat source? Natural gas is typically cheaper than electric or propane. You must also consider how many appliances are currently running from that source. Switching an electric dryer to a gas dryer or vice versa could reduce your monthly bill.

3. Is there a gas well on the property? This can be a significant cost savings! If you're in an area rich in natural gas, there may be many properties that have natural gas storage or production wells. Typically, these wells have agreements that provide free gas to the property and even potentially a yearly payout. I currently have a property with a gas storage well that provides free gas to the home on the property and pays $200 per year. By having all the appliances running on gas and not having a water, sewage, or water runoff bill, the utility costs are minimal.

4. Who is the electric provider? Knowing who the electric provider is, you can look up their current rates and determine how much you may have to pay monthly. You may be able to choose the electric generation supplier and lock in a low fixed rate for a specific term.

5. If there is a gas line, where is it, and where is the meter? Most of the time, the homeowner is responsible for the gas line from the meter into the home. That means if it has issues over time, you will be responsible for fixing it. This is the same whether you are in the city or the country. If the meter is far from the home, you may have much of the line you are responsible for.

6. Is there a gas or electric transmission line or other utilities running through the property with easements? If utilities run through the property, you may have limited use of some of the property where their easement lies. This may also mean that you have a right to service from that company.

These questions don't capture absolutely everything but are a good starting point and will get you thinking about things most people will overlook.

Internet and Communications

Urban residents typically enjoy a variety of options for internet and communication services, including high-speed fiber optic, cable, and DSL. Competition among providers in urban areas helps to keep prices relatively competitive, and service reliability is generally high. Recently, I switched from cable to fiber and noticed a much higher upload speed. Download speeds are about the same and costs are slightly different. Anything is better than the dial-up we had when I was younger.

In **Rural** areas, Internet access remains one of the biggest challenges. Many rural regions lack high-speed internet options and service can be expensive and unreliable. Satellite internet is commonly available but can be slower and more susceptible to weather disturbances—recent initiatives and investments in rural broadband infrastructure aim to improve this. One big one is Elon Musk's Star Link. They have been making significant strides in the quality and speed you can get from satellite internet. I expect they will soon rival most other internet providers as they continue to launch more satellites into orbit.

Overall Cost and Accessibility

Urban residents often face higher monthly utility costs due to higher water, sewage, and energy rates, compounded by cities' higher cost of living. Rural residents might benefit from lower monthly fees but must contend with higher upfront costs for installing and maintaining independent systems.

Urban settings offer the convenience of immediate professional service for repairs and maintenance. At the same time, rural homeowners may find fewer service providers and longer wait times for repairs, often at a premium cost due to the travel distance for technicians.

Understanding the differences is crucial for anyone considering a move or looking to optimize their living arrangements. Each setting requires different strategies for managing utility costs and ensuring a sustainable, comfortable living environment.

THE 2-YEAR STRATEGY

The 2-Year Strategy is a tactical approach to real estate that leverages the tax advantages available to homeowners who utilize their property not just as a residence but as a financial tool. This strategy hinges on the understanding of specific tax laws that exempt homeowners from capital gains taxes on their primary residence if they've lived in the home for two of the five years preceding the sale. Here's how you can apply this approach to amplify your financial growth and navigate the real estate market more adeptly. Combining this strategy with House Hacking can take it even one step further. You could ramp up savings and eventually build a portfolio of real estate that provides monthly cash flow for you. Either way, the 2-year strategy is a powerful tool you can use to create extra wealth.

Understanding the Tax Benefits The cornerstone of the 2-Year Strategy lies in capitalizing on the IRS Section 121 exclusion, which allows individuals to exclude up to $250,000 ($500,000 for married couples) in capital gains on real estate if they have used the house as their primary residence for at least two out of the last five years before selling. This exemption can be used multiple times throughout your life, but not more frequently than once every two years.

Selecting the Right Property The key to success with the 2-Year Strategy is choosing a property that will appreciate in value during your time of ownership. Look for homes in emerging neighborhoods or areas expected to appreciate due to economic or developmental changes. Properties that require some upgrades or minor renovations are also ideal, as they allow for forced appreciation through improvements. This often leads to a higher sale price, which is the goal.

Implementing Sweat Equity 'Sweat equity' refers to enhancing a property's value through your own labor, aside from financial investment. This could involve DIY home improvements like painting, upgrading fixtures, landscaping, and other renovations that increase the property's market value without requiring substantial capital. The upgrades not only make the property more enjoyable while you live there but also boost its value when you're ready to sell. The more work the property needs, the better deal you will get when purchasing and the more equity you can drive into it to capitalize on when you sell.

Strategic Considerations for Buying and Selling Timing your purchase and subsequent sale around the two-year mark is crucial. However, it's essential to remain flexible, as market conditions can change. Keeping a close eye on local market trends and getting regular property valuations can inform the best time to sell. Additionally, understanding the local real estate market helps in purchasing properties that are likely to provide the best return on investment.

Financial Planning and Execution While living in the property, planning financially for the eventual sale is beneficial. This means setting aside a budget for necessary improvements and considering mortgage payments that will allow for flexibility in pricing when you decide to sell. Effective financial management ensures you're not over-leveraged, maintaining enough liquidity to handle unforeseen expenses or market shifts.

The 2-Year Strategy is not just about finding a place to live; it's about intelligent investing and strategic planning. By understanding and utilizing tax laws to your advantage, choosing the right property and adding value through improvements, you can significantly enhance your finances or portfolio through real estate. This approach requires diligence and a proactive stance in managing your investment but offers substantial financial rewards that can accelerate your journey toward financial independence.

Check out this example and break down a deal using the strategy:

Clara and Alex, a couple in their early thirties, recently used the 2-Year Strategy to significantly boost their financial standing. They purchased a moderately priced fixer-upper in a promising neighborhood of Austin, Texas, known for its rapid growth and development.

Initial Purchase:

- **Purchase Price:** $300,000
- **Down Payment:** $60,000 (20% of the purchase price)
- **Mortgage Details:** $240,000 mortgage at 4% interest rate
- **Monthly Mortgage Payment:** Approximately $1,146

Renovation and Improvement Costs:

- **Total Investment in Improvements:** $40,000 (including kitchen remodel, bathroom updates, and landscaping)

Total Initial Investment:

- **Down Payment + Improvements:** $100,000

Living and Improving: Clara and Alex lived in the home over the next two years while making gradual improvements. They focused on cost-effective upgrades offering the highest return on investment, such as modernizing the main living areas and improving the home's curb appeal.

Sale of the Home:

- **Sale Price After Two Years:** $450,000
- **Capital Gains:** $150,000

Calculating the Profit:

- **Cost Basis (Purchase Price + Improvements):** $340,000
- **Selling Price:** $450,000
- **Profit:** $110,000 after closing costs and realtor fees (approximately $10,000)

Capital Gains Tax Savings:

- Since Clara and Alex lived in the property as their primary residence for two out of the five years preceding the sale, they qualified for the IRS Section 121 exclusion. This allowed them to exclude up to $500,000 of capital gains as a married couple, so they owed no capital gains tax on their profit.

Net Gain:

- **Total Gain from the Sale:** $110,000
- This profit was **tax-free**, substantially adding to their financial assets.

Clara and Alex's story illustrates how effectively the 2-Year Strategy can be leveraged to generate significant financial gains through intelligent real estate investments and timely improvements. Their initial $100,000 investment turned into a $110,000 profit in just two years, demonstrating the power of strategic planning and understanding of real estate market dynamics. This example serves as a compelling case for the potential financial benefits of combining homeownership with strategic investment, particularly for individuals willing to invest sweat equity into their properties.

Had Clara and Alex used an FHA loan, they probably could have purchased the home for 3% down ($9,000) and completed the strategy with much less money involved. There are many ways you can do this without having to save up a ton of money. Another fantastic option is an FHA 203k loan. We will cover financing options in Chapter 6 in detail. Hopefully, by now, you can see how powerful this strategy can be and how you can use it to get yourself started on a new path towards prosperity!

Bringing It All Together

This chapter has explored a variety of strategies that not only facilitate relocating for financial gain but also empower you to maximize your income through strategic moves. From employer-paid relocation packages to incentive programs offered by cities and states and the practical considerations of managing utilities and employing the 2-Year Strategy in real estate, we've covered a broad spectrum of opportunities that can significantly enhance your financial landscape.

While often daunting, relocation presents unique financial opportunities that can lead to substantial savings and earning potential. Employer relocation packages can offset the costs and stresses associated with moving for a job, while various city and state incentive programs across the country offer compelling reasons to consider such moves, including financial bonuses and ongoing tax breaks.

Additionally, the 2-Year Strategy discussed provides a clear, actionable plan for leveraging real estate investments in conjunction with relocation to maximize returns. Understanding and utilizing these strategies allows you to turn what often seems like a mere life change into a powerful financial growth opportunity.

As we conclude this chapter, remember that each move and financial decision should be tailored to your circumstances, career goals, and financial objectives. Whether you are moving across the state or the country, the strategies outlined here aim to equip you with the knowledge to make informed decisions that align with your long-term financial prosperity.

Embark on your journey confidently, knowing that "Moving for Money" isn't just about changing where you live—it's about strategically enhancing your financial well-being.

THE LESSER-KNOWN PATH TO FINANCIAL FREEDOM

Financial freedom is freedom from fear.

— ROBERT KIYOSAKI

We hear a lot about property investment as a route to financial freedom, but moving for money is rarely mentioned. The vast majority of people don't realize how much money can be saved (and made) from strategic relocation, so it isn't even a consideration. I'm not here to try to tell everyone they should move; my goal is to spread this information so that more people have a real shot at whipping their financial health into shape and getting themselves closer to financial freedom.

Ultimately, what we all care about is having a fulfilling life and enough freedom to be able to enjoy it. Money may not be the answer to all of our problems, but it's certainly a way to reach those very reasonable goals. That's something we all deserve a shot at – and people all over the world are searching for ways to do it.

You only have to type the first part of the sentence, "How to become financially free" into Google to see that it's a question many people are looking to find answers to, yet I know they're not finding all the in-roads they could be... and strategic relocation is a powerful one. I'm determined to share this information as widely as I can to help people make fully informed decisions and make the choices that will really make a difference to their bank balances. It is, I feel, a worthy cause... and you can be a part of it. All you have to do is leave a short review.

By leaving a review of this book on Amazon, you'll show new readers where they can find all the information they need to learn about this often-overlooked approach to making money.

They're searching for solutions, and strategic relocation is one they'll rarely find unless we up the discourse about it and help people find the information they need to understand it. Your review will help to do that.

I want to make a real difference in the world and to do it I'm going to need your help. Thank you so much for your support.

Scan the QR code below

REMOTE WORK AND GEOGRAPHIC ARBITRAGE

" *The world is a book and those who do not travel read only one page.*

— SAINT AUGUSTINE

As the work landscape undergoes its most significant transformation in decades, remote work has emerged not just as a temporary solution but as a permanent fixture in the professional world. This shift from traditional office environments towards more flexible working arrangements presents unique opportunities and challenges, especially regarding personal finance and lifestyle choices. This chapter explores the financial benefits and broader implications of remote work, exploring how it can reshape your economic landscape and enhance your quality of life.

Understanding these elements will give you the knowledge to navigate the new norms of employment and maximize your financial well-being in the era of remote work. Whether you're a seasoned remote worker or considering a transition, this chapter will provide valuable insights into making the most of remote work from a financial perspective.

THE FINANCIAL BENEFITS OF REMOTE WORK

In the evolving work landscape, remote employment has emerged as a transformative force, not only in how we work but also in how we manage our finances. The shift towards remote work offers numerous financial benefits, enhancing direct savings and income opportunities, significant tax advantages and improved work-life balance. Here's a deeper look at these aspects:

Cost Savings One of the most immediate benefits of remote work is the significant reduction in commuting costs. Without the daily drive or ride to an office, you save on gas, public transit fares, car maintenance and parking fees. But the savings extend beyond just commuting. Working from home reduces the need for a professional wardrobe, a substantial expense in many industries. Additionally, remote work often means home-cooked meals, which are generally cheaper than lunches bought near the office or business lunches.

Income Opportunities Remote work breaks down geographic barriers, opening up a world of employment opportunities previously restricted by location. This accessibility allows for seeking positions in higher-paying markets without needing to relocate, leading to significantly higher income potential. It also provides the flexibility to take on freelance gigs or side projects that can supplement your primary income, leveraging skills that might not be as marketable in your local geographical job market.

Tax Implications For remote workers, potential tax deductions can make a notable difference in annual tax responsibilities. If you use a portion of your home exclusively for business purposes, you may be eligible to claim the home office deduction, which can include a portion of utilities, property taxes, and mortgage interest or rent. However, compliance with IRS rules is essential to qualify for these deductions. Additionally, the state tax implications of remote work can vary significantly; some states have tax reciprocity agreements, while others may require you to file multiple state tax returns if you live in one state and your employer is based in another, potentially affecting your overall tax liability.

Work-Life Balance Beyond financial metrics, remote work offers invaluable benefits in terms of work-life balance, which can indirectly contribute to financial savings. With more control over your schedule, you can manage time more effectively, reducing stress and potentially decreasing healthcare costs associated with burnout and other stress-related conditions. Integrating work with personal life more smoothly can lead to higher job satisfaction and productivity, which are beneficial for career progression.

NAVIGATING THE REAL ESTATE MARKET: WHEN TO RENT VS. BUY

In remote work, where location flexibility is a key advantage, deciding whether to rent or buy becomes an essential consideration in financial planning. This decision can significantly impact your financial health, depending on your career stability, lifestyle preferences, and your chosen locale's real estate market dynamics. Here's a detailed exploration of the advantages of renting versus buying in the era of remote work, along with guidance on navigating these options effectively.

Advantages of Renting offers flexibility that is particularly valuable in today's ever-changing job market. For remote workers considering future relocations or not ready to commit to a single location, renting can be a wise choice. The ability to move without the complexities of selling a property is a significant benefit. Financially, renting requires less upfront investment compared to buying a home, as it avoids the substantial down payment and additional costs such as property taxes, home insurance, and maintenance expenses. This can be particularly advantageous for those who prefer to invest their savings in other areas with potentially higher returns.

Advantages of Buying Owning a home, on the other hand, is traditionally seen as a sound investment that can contribute to long-term financial security. Buying a home can make more economic sense for remote workers with stable jobs and a desire to stay in one location for an extended period. Homeownership locks in your monthly payments if you opt for a fixed-rate mortgage, protecting you from annual rent increases. Additionally, building equity in a home can be a powerful tool for wealth accumulation, especially in real estate markets with rising property values. The tax benefits, such as deductions on mortgage interest and property taxes, also provide significant financial incentives for buyers.

Market Considerations The decision to rent or buy should also consider current real estate market conditions. In markets where housing prices are exceptionally high, the immediate costs of buying may not outweigh the long-term benefits, making renting a more sensible option. In areas where the market is more affordable, the investment in buying a home could promise great appreciation over time.

Personal Factors Beyond financial and market considerations, individual factors are crucial in this decision. These include your financial readiness, income stability, lifestyle preferences, and willingness to engage in home maintenance and improvement projects. For remote workers, considerations might also include the need for a suitable home office space and the potential for that space to influence home-buying decisions.

COST OF LIVING ADJUSTMENTS: MAXIMIZING YOUR MONEY WHERE YOU LIVE

Remote work offers the flexibility to choose where you work and the opportunity to strategically select a living location that maximizes your financial potential. This section discusses the concept of cost-of-living adjustments (COLA), how to effectively compare the cost of living between different areas, and the financial advantages of relocating to a less expensive area.

Understanding COLA Cost-of-living adjustments refer to the changes employers make to salaries based on geographic area to ensure that employees' purchasing power remains consistent despite varying costs of living. Understanding COLA is crucial for remote workers, especially if they are considering a move or negotiating salaries with employers in different cities. However, many remote positions may offer a standard salary regardless of location, leading workers to seek areas where they can maximize their income by minimizing living costs.

Comparing Cost of Living When considering a move, it's essential to compare the cost-of-living indices between your current location and potential new homes. These indices take into account various factors such as housing costs, groceries, healthcare, utilities, transportation and more. Several online tools and resources can provide detailed comparisons. For instance, websites like Numbeo, Expatistan, and the Cost of Living Index by the Council for Community and Economic Research (C2ER) offer comprehensive data that can help remote workers make informed decisions.

Relocation for Lower Cost of Living Relocating to an area with a lower cost of living can significantly enhance your financial well-being. This strategy is particularly effective for remote workers whose employers do not adjust pay based on location. Moving from a high-cost city to a more affordable small town or rural area can reduce your expenses dramatically, especially in housing costs. This reduction in fixed expenses can free up funds for savings, investment, and discretionary spending, potentially leading to a better quality of life.

Budget Adjustments After relocating, it's crucial to adjust your budget to reflect the new cost of living. This might mean reallocating funds previously spent on expensive urban rent or mortgages towards savings, retirement, or lifestyle enhancements like travel and hobbies. It's also essential to account for any new expenses that may arise in a new location, such as increased travel costs for visiting family or higher costs for services that were cheaper in urban areas.

For remote workers, strategically choosing where to live can be as crucial as career choices in maximizing financial potential. Understanding and leveraging the differences in cost of living can significantly enhance your financial flexibility and quality of life. Having the right tools to assess and compare these costs and understand the broader economic implications of your relocation choices enable you to make decisions that align with your personal and financial goals.

MAKING A NEW CITY FEEL LIKE HOME: SOCIAL TIPS AND COMMUNITY ENGAGEMENT

Transitioning to a new city, whether for remote work flexibility, financial reasons, or personal growth, can be exciting and daunting. While the logistical aspects of such a move, like housing and utilities, are critical, integrating into your new environment socially and culturally is equally essential for making your new city feel like home. Here are some strategies to help you settle in and thrive in your new surroundings by building connections and engaging with the community.

Building a New Social Network Creating a new social circle in a new city can make the transition smoother and more enjoyable:

- **Attend Local Events and Meetups**: Look for events that align with your interests on platforms like Meetup.com or local community boards. Whether it's a book club, a hiking group, or a tech meetup, these gatherings provide excellent opportunities to meet people with similar interests.
- **Leverage Social Media and Apps**: Platforms like Facebook, Nextdoor, and Bumble BFF can be helpful in connecting with neighbors and joining community groups. These tools offer a direct way to engage with local events, community projects, and other social gatherings.

- **Volunteer**: Volunteering for a local charity, nonprofit, or community organization is fulfilling and a great way to meet people and learn more about the priorities and culture of your new city.

Engaging with the Community Deepening your connection with the community can enhance your sense of belonging:

- **Participate in Local Government and Civic Initiatives**: Attend city council meetings, school board meetings, or community planning events to understand local issues and contribute your voice and efforts to community development.
- **Support Local Businesses**: Frequent local shops, restaurants, and markets to build relationships with local business owners and residents. This supports the local economy and helps you integrate into the community's economic fabric.
- **Join Local Clubs and Societies**: Whether it's a sports league, a gardening club, or a historical society, joining a club can connect you with like-minded individuals and give you a regular activity to look forward to.

Exploring and Learning About Your New City Become an explorer in your city and discover what makes it unique:

- **Tourist for a Day**: Spend a day visiting major tourist attractions to understand your new home's cultural and historical context. This can provide conversation starters and deepen your appreciation for your new city.
- **Cultural Immersion**: Attend local festivals, concerts, and art exhibits to immerse yourself in the local culture. This

can also expand your understanding of the diverse communities within the city.

- **Culinary Adventures**: Explore local cuisine through restaurants and food markets. Food is a central part of cultural identity and can be a delightful way to experience the diversity of your new home.

Adjusting to Cultural Differences, Especially if moving to a significantly different region or country:

- **Cultural Sensitivity Training**: If available, participate in cultural sensitivity training or workshops to understand your new home's social norms and cultural nuances.
- **Language Classes**: If moving to an area with a different predominant language, language classes can help you communicate more effectively and integrate better into the community.

Moving to a new city is a rich journey that offers both challenges and rewards. By actively seeking ways to connect socially, engage with the community, and immerse yourself in local culture, you can transform any new city into a place you can proudly call home.

Here are five questions designed to deepen your understanding of the concepts covered in this chapter. They are meant to prompt you to reflect on how these concepts apply to your personal and professional life. By contemplating your answers, you can gauge your readiness and identify areas where you might need more planning or research. This process of self-reflection and planning empowers you to make more informed decisions, taking control of your journey to a new city.

1. **Cost Comparison**: List three major cities you would consider moving to. Compare the cost of living in these cities to your current city. Which city offers the best financial advantages considering your remote work salary?
2. **Tax Implications**: What are the potential tax implications of working remotely from a different state than your employer's base? How can these affect your net income?
3. **Housing Decisions**: Based on your current lifestyle and financial goals, would renting or buying a home be more advantageous if you moved to a lower-cost area? Explain your reasoning.
4. **Community Engagement**: What are three ways you could start building a new social network and engage with the community if you moved to a new city? How important is community integration to your sense of well-being?
5. **Cultural Adaptation**: If moving to a city with a significantly different cultural background from yours, what steps would you take to ensure a smooth adaptation?

This chapter has explored the multifaceted financial and lifestyle considerations of remote work and geographic arbitrage. From understanding the economic impacts of living in different locales to navigating the real estate market, from tax implications to integrating into a new community, the flexibility of remote work offers unique opportunities to significantly enhance one's financial health and quality of life, instilling a sense of optimism and hope for a brighter future.

As the world of work continues to evolve, leveraging the strategies discussed in this chapter can position you to make informed decisions that align with your personal and financial goals. Whether you choose to move to a more cost-effective area or decide to explore new cultural horizons, the ability to work remotely can be a powerful tool in crafting a fulfilling and financially stable life.

Reflect on the questions above and consider how the answers might influence your decisions in the future. Each step in this journey offers a chance to improve your financial standing and enriches your life with new experiences and insights. Embrace the possibilities of remote work and continue seeking knowledge and strategies to support your journey to financial independence and personal satisfaction.

FINANCING

Financial freedom is available to those who learn about it and work for it.

— ROBERT KIYOSAKI

Navigating the financing landscape is a pivotal step in your journey toward homeownership. This chapter breaks down the complex world of home loans, providing you with the knowledge to make informed decisions about financing your new home. Whether you're a first-time buyer or looking to refinance, understanding the nuances of various mortgage options will empower you to choose a loan that best suits your financial goals and lifestyle needs. From the mechanics behind different types of mortgages to exploring eligibility criteria and the intricacies of the application process, this chapter lays a solid foundation for securing your financial future through intelligent borrowing.

UNDERSTANDING YOUR MORTGAGE OPTIONS - A COMPREHENSIVE GUIDE

When entering the world of home financing, choosing the right mortgage can have a lasting impact on your financial health and how much you pay over time. Let's explore the various types of mortgages available, including fixed-rate, adjustable-rate, and government-backed loans, providing a clear path through this complex landscape.

Conventional Loans: A conventional loan is a type of mortgage that is not backed by the government. These loans typically require a higher down payment than FHA loans but may offer more flexible terms and lower interest rates. Conventional loans can be a good option for investors who have a larger down payment saved up and want to minimize their monthly mortgage payments.

Fixed-Rate Mortgages (FRM) A fixed-rate mortgage offers the stability of consistent interest rates and monthly payments throughout the life of the loan, which can typically last 15, 20, or 30 years. This predictability makes budgeting easier and shields borrowers from rising interest rates, making it ideal for those who plan on making their new house a long-term home.

Pros:

- **Stability and Predictability:** The primary advantage of a fixed-rate mortgage is its stability. Your interest rate and monthly mortgage payments remain the same throughout the loan's term, making budgeting more straightforward and predictable.
- **Inflation Protection:** As inflation rises, your mortgage payments become cheaper over time due to the fixed interest rate.
- **Simplicity:** Fixed-rate mortgages are straightforward and easy to understand, making them a good choice for first-time homebuyers.

Cons:

- **Higher Initial Rates:** Fixed-rate mortgages typically start with a higher interest rate than adjustable-rate mortgages, meaning higher initial monthly payments.
- **Less Flexibility:** If interest rates fall, homeowners with fixed-rate mortgages may miss out on the opportunity to benefit from lower rates unless they refinance, which involves additional costs and hassle.

Adjustable-Rate Mortgages (ARM) Adjustable-rate mortgages initially provide a lower interest rate, which adjusts at pre-defined periods based on market trends. These adjustments are linked to a specific index plus a set margin. While ARMs often offer lower rates at the beginning, making them attractive during periods of high interest rates, they carry the risk of significant increases in payments over time if interest rates rise. They are best suited for those who plan to move or refinance before the rate adjusts or can accommodate higher future payments.

Pros:

- **Lower Initial Rates:** ARMs often offer lower initial rates than fixed-rate mortgages, which can save money in the short term and make qualifying for a loan easier.
- **Potential for Decreased Rates:** If interest rates fall, you might benefit without refinancing, as the rate adjustment could lead to lower payments.
- **Cap on Adjustments:** Most ARMs have caps that limit the increase in the interest rate or monthly payment, offering some protection against drastic rate increases.

Cons:

- **Rate and Payment Uncertainty:** The biggest drawback of an ARM is the uncertainty. After the initial fixed period, the interest rate can fluctuate based on the market, which can lead to significantly higher payments.
- **Complexity:** The terms and conditions of ARMs (including caps, margins, and adjustment indices) can be complex and challenging for many homebuyers to understand.

HELOC: A home equity line of credit (HELOC) is a type of loan that allows borrowers to borrow against the equity in their home. This can be a good option for investors who already own a property and want to use the equity to finance a house hack. HELOCs typically have higher interest rates than other types of loans and may require a higher credit score and more equity in the property. This would probably be one of my last picks as the interest rate will likely be higher than a conventional mortgage. HELOCs are a good option for short-term use, such as flipping a house.

Pros:

- **Flexibility in Use and Repayment:** A HELOC offers significant flexibility, allowing you to borrow as much or as little as you need up to the credit limit during the draw period. This makes it ideal for ongoing projects or expenses such as home renovations, education costs, or medical bills. You can also choose interest-only payments during the draw period, easing financial burden when funds are tight.
- **Potential Tax Benefits:** The interest paid on a HELOC may be tax-deductible if the loan is used to buy, build, or substantially improve the taxpayer's home that secures the loan. This can reduce the overall cost of borrowing, but it's essential to consult with a tax advisor to understand how it applies to your situation.
- **Lower Interest Rates Than Some Loans:** Typically, HELOCs have lower interest rates compared to credit cards and personal loans. This is because the loan is secured by your home, making it less risky for lenders. Lower rates can result in significant savings over the life of the loan.

Cons:

- **Risk of Foreclosure:** Because a HELOC is secured by your home, failing to meet repayment obligations can lead to foreclosure. It's crucial to manage borrowing and ensure that repayments are within your financial capacity, especially considering that interest rates on HELOCs can fluctuate, potentially increasing your payment amounts.
- **Variable Interest Rates:** Most HELOCs have variable interest rates, which means the interest cost can increase

or decrease based on market changes. This variability can make it challenging to predict monthly payments and plan finances long-term, potentially leading to payment shock if rates rise significantly.

- **Complexity and Potential for Overborrowing:** The flexibility of a HELOC can also be a downside if not managed carefully. The ability to draw funds over time can lead to overspending, and borrowers might find themselves using their homes as ATMs, jeopardizing financial stability. Additionally, the terms and conditions of HELOCs, including the repayment schedule and handling of the end of the draw period, can be complex and confusing for some homeowners.

Government-Backed Loans These loans are designed to make home-buying more accessible:

Pros:

- **Lower Down Payments:** Government-backed loans, such as FHA and USDA loans, often require lower down payments than conventional loans. In some cases, no down payment is required at all, like USDA and VA loans.
- **Easier Qualification:** These loans are generally easier to qualify for, with more lenient credit scores and debt-to-income ratio requirements.
- **Additional Features:** Programs like the FHA 203(k) provide funding for both purchase and renovation in a single loan, expanding home-buying options for properties that need work. This would be a go-to option if you're looking for a fixer-upper.

Cons:

- **Mortgage Insurance Requirements:** Besides VA loans, government-backed loans require borrowers to pay mortgage insurance premiums, which can add to the monthly cost of the loan.
- **Limited Availability:** Some government-backed loans restrict the type of property you can buy or where it must be located (as with USDA loans).
- **Longer Processing Times:** Due to additional paperwork and requirements, the approval process for these loans can sometimes be longer than for a conventional mortgage.

FHA Loans: Known for their lower down payment requirements and more accessible credit qualifications, FHA loans are a popular choice among first-time homebuyers.

VA Loans: Available to veterans, active-duty service members, and certain members of the National Guard and reserves, VA loans are notable for not requiring a down payment or private mortgage insurance (PMI). This can lead to significant savings upfront and over the duration of the loan.

USDA Loans: Targeted at homebuyers in rural areas, USDA loans offer 100% financing, meaning no down payment is required, along with reduced mortgage insurance rates and below-market mortgage rates.

Each type of government-backed loan is designed with the borrower's needs in mind, offering various benefits to lower the barriers to homeownership. For example, the FHA 203(k) program is particularly beneficial for buyers interested in purchasing fixer-uppers, as it provides the funds needed for acquisition and renovation in a single loan. I used this type of loan for my first house, which I bought as a foreclosure. I would highly recommend looking into this option, as you could end up with a lot of equity in your home.

ELIGIBILITY

Understanding the eligibility requirements for various types of mortgages is crucial for prospective homebuyers as it helps determine which loan best fits individual financial circumstances. Here's an overview of what you need to qualify for fixed-rate mortgages, adjustable-rate mortgages, and several government-backed loans.

For **Fixed-Rate Mortgages (FRM)**, lenders typically look for a minimum credit score of 620, though a score of 740 or higher may secure better interest rates. The standard down payment is usually 20% of the home's purchase price to avoid the additional cost of private mortgage insurance (PMI). However, lower down payments are possible but require PMI, increasing the monthly payment. Lenders generally prefer a debt-to-income ratio (DTI) of 43% or less, and borrowers must provide proof of stable and verifiable income through employment documents, pay stubs, and tax returns. I have completed several conventional fixed-rate mortgages with a 5% down payment without issues.

Adjustable-Rate Mortgages (ARM) share similar credit score requirements to FRMs, but some lenders may apply stricter standards due to the potential for increasing payments. The down payment for an ARM varies by lender and loan terms, typically starting at 5%. A DTI of 43% or lower is also preferred for ARMs, with proof of stable income and employment essential to accommodate the uncertainty of future rate adjustments.

Government-backed loans offer more flexible terms to encourage homeownership. **FHA Loans** require a credit score of at least 580 for a 3.5% down payment or 500 with a 10% down payment. FHA loans accept higher DTI ratios, up to 50%, and require mortgage insurance regardless of the down payment size. **VA Loans**, available to veterans and certain military members, do not specify a minimum credit score but most lenders prefer 620. VA loans offer the significant benefit of requiring no down payment and typically favor a DTI ratio of 41%, although there is flexibility depending on other factors.

USDA Loans are geared towards buyers in rural areas and have specific property and income eligibility requirements. Homes must be in USDA-approved areas, and borrowers' income must not exceed 115% of the median area income. A credit score of 640 is generally preferred for more straightforward processing, though lower scores may be considered with additional underwriting. The USDA also typically requires a DTI ratio of 41% or less, with possible allowances of up to 44% for applicants with solid credit backgrounds.

Choosing between these mortgage options requires a thorough assessment of your financial situation, future plans, and how much risk you are willing to take on. Whether you value stability in your monthly payments or are looking for lower initial rates to save on immediate costs, understanding the nuances of each mortgage type will guide you in selecting the best option for securing your financial future while achieving your dream of homeownership. A good mortgage broker should be able to help point you in the right direction and get you the best interest rate and loan for your situation.

PERSONAL FINANCING EXPERIENCE

In my experience purchasing different types of real estate, I have used a few types of loans. The first property I purchased was a foreclosure and I used an FHA 203K loan to buy and fix up the house and prepare it to move into. This allowed me to use a loan for the purchase and the rehab. Once a contractor was selected and approved by the bank, they would complete inspections during the renovation to approve draws by the contractor and pay for the work that had been completed. I have heard some negatives about these loans from various people, but it worked out well for me. If memory serves me right, I believe I put a 3-5% down payment on this loan to get approved. Overall, it was a smooth process. A year later, I found another property to buy that put me closer to work, and I was able to sell my first property for an almost $40K profit. Being that it was my primary residence and I was moving a certain minimum distance to relocate for work, I did not have to pay ANY taxes on the gains from the sale. This is also true if you have lived in a property as your primary residence for any 2 years in the previous 5 years. We discussed this 2-year strategy in more detail previously. Refer to that section for more information.

I have purchased some of my properties using a conventional loan with a 5% down payment. If you can afford a little extra on the down payment, this loan process is a little simpler than an FHA loan and more flexible. Also, sellers are more apt to accept a conventional loan offer than an FHA loan offer due to the extra stipulations and inspections that come with FHA. Keep that in mind when you're house hunting in a hot market and there's a potential for multiple offers as the sellers will likely favor a conventional offer.

Another way I was able to purchase rental property was with a cash offer, using a HELOC (home equity line of credit) that I had on my primary residence. Once I bought the property and completed renovations, I completed a cash-out refinance on the property and paid off the HELOC. That put a 30-year loan on the rental and I then had access to the funds on my HELOC again and could repeat the process if needed. Also note that once the property was fully rented, it was cash-flowing $1,000 per month! That's after paying the new mortgage, taxes and insurance. It probably wouldn't be a good idea to use this strategy if the property you are purchasing is not going to cash flow or you are not planning to move into it yourself.

Lastly, I have used commercial financing to buy apartments. These terms can vary and these loans are typically for buildings with more than four units. You can use traditional financing for buildings with up to four units. This required a 20% down payment and was an adjustable-rate mortgage. Luckily, we sold this property for a great profit before the major interest rate hikes, which would have hit us and decreased the property's value!

These are just a few examples of my real-world experience using different kinds of financing to buy property. Remember always to do your due diligence and find what option will work best for you and your situation. As stated previously, a good mortgage broker should be able to help guide you through the process and point you in the right direction.

DSCR LOANS

One type of financing option that I haven't used yet but can be a great tool is a **DSCR** loan. A Debt Service Coverage Ratio (DSCR) loan is a type of investment property loan that primarily relies on the cash flow generated by the property to determine eligibility rather than the borrower's income. DSCR loans are desirable for real estate investors who might not qualify for traditional mortgages due to variable income or owning multiple properties.

The key metric in a DSCR loan is the Debt Service Coverage Ratio itself, which is calculated by dividing the property's annual net operating income (NOI) by its annual mortgage debt service (total of principal and interest payments). Essentially, the DSCR measures the cash flow available to pay the current debt obligations related to the property:

DSCR=Net Operating Income (NOI) /Debt Service

Net Operating Income (NOI): The property's gross rental income minus operating expenses (not including the mortgage payment). Operating expenses include property management fees, property taxes, insurance, and maintenance costs.

Ideal DSCR Values

- A DSCR of 1.0 means the net operating income equals the annual debt payments — you're breaking even, which is generally the minimum most lenders will consider.
- A DSCR greater than 1.0 indicates that there is more income than the debt service requirement, which is favorable for lenders. For example, a DSCR of 1.25 means that the property generates 25% more revenue than is needed to cover the debt payments.
- Conversely, a DSCR below 1.0 means the property does not generate enough income to cover the debt service, which most lenders would view as risky.

How DSCR Loans are Used to Purchase Property

DSCR loans are used by real estate investors looking to purchase or refinance rental properties without relying on personal income documentation. Instead, the loan underwriting process focuses on the property's income-producing potential. Here's how they are typically used:

1. **Investment Property Purchase**: Investors use DSCR loans to buy properties they intend to rent out. The rental income must be sufficient to cover the mortgage and other costs associated with maintaining the property.
2. **Refinancing**: Property owners might refinance existing mortgages with a DSCR loan to secure better terms based on the current income of the property, especially if their financial situation has changed.
3. **Portfolio Expansion**: For real estate investors looking to expand their portfolios without the constraints of traditional mortgage qualifications tied to personal income, DSCR loans provide a pathway to leverage property cash flows for further acquisitions.

Advantages and Considerations

- **Less Personal Financial Scrutiny**: Since the loan approval is primarily based on the property's income, there is less focus on the borrower's income, debt-to-income ratio, or credit score.
- **Quick Closings**: Because DSCR loans require less personal financial information to process, closing can be quicker than traditional loans.
- **Higher Interest Rates and Down Payments**: Because DSCR loans often represent a higher risk to lenders, they

typically have higher interest rates and down payment requirements than traditional mortgages.

DSCR loans offer real estate investors a valuable financing tool, enabling them to leverage property income for growth opportunities. However, it's crucial to thoroughly understand the cost implications and ensure the property investment offers sufficient cash flow to comfortably meet loan obligations.

MORTGAGE CALCULATORS

When navigating the complex world of mortgages, online mortgage calculators are invaluable tools that can simplify your decision-making process. These calculators help you estimate your monthly mortgage payments and compare different options, providing a clearer picture of what you can afford and how different variables affect your payments.

Mortgage calculators are user-friendly digital tools available on numerous financial websites, including banks, mortgage companies, and personal finance sites. You can receive an instant estimate of your potential monthly mortgage payment by inputting details such as the home price, down payment, loan term, interest rate, and sometimes additional costs like property taxes, homeowners' association fees, and insurance. For some quick numbers, I sometimes use the Zillow app.

Benefits of Using Mortgage Calculators

1. **Budget Planning:** One of the primary advantages of using a mortgage calculator is its role in budget planning. It allows you to play with different scenarios and see how changes in down payment amounts or

loan terms can affect your monthly expenses. This flexibility helps you set realistic expectations and determine how much of a house you can afford based on your budget.

2. **Comparing Loan Options:** Mortgage calculators can compare various mortgage types side by side. Whether deciding between a 15-year and a 30-year fixed mortgage or comparing fixed-rate mortgages against adjustable-rate mortgages, these tools can show you how each option impacts your finances in the long term.

3. **Interest Calculations:** Understanding how much of your monthly payment goes towards interest versus principal is crucial. Mortgage calculators often break down each payment so you can see how your payments decrease the principal over the years and how much total interest you will pay over the life of the loan.

4. **Saving Money:** By testing different scenarios, such as making extra payments, you can find strategies to save money on interest. This can significantly reduce the life of your loan and total interest paid, helping you build equity faster.

How to Use Mortgage Calculators Effectively

To make the most of mortgage calculators, ensure you have accurate and realistic input values:

- **Interest Rates:** Use current market rates based on your credit score and general market conditions.
- **Home Price:** Enter the price range you are considering based on your market research and real estate trends.
- **Down Payment:** Adjust the down payment to see how it affects monthly payments and whether you'll need PMI.

- **Loan Terms:** Experiment with different terms to balance monthly affordability and total interest paid.

Remember, while mortgage calculators provide a good estimation, they may not always include all costs associated with a mortgage, such as closing costs or fluctuating property taxes. For a comprehensive understanding, it's advisable to consult with a mortgage advisor who can provide detailed insights and help tailor a mortgage strategy to your financial situation. Incorporating mortgage calculators into your homebuying process empowers you to make informed, strategic decisions about your mortgage, allowing you to manage your finances wisely as you step into homeownership.

HOW TO QUALIFY FOR A MORTGAGE: TIPS AND TRICKS

Securing a mortgage is a crucial step on the path to homeownership. Enhancing your financial profile and understanding the qualification criteria can significantly improve your chances of obtaining favorable mortgage terms. Here are some essential strategies to prepare you effectively for the mortgage application process.

Improving Your Credit Score Your credit score significantly influences the interest rates and terms you'll receive on a mortgage. Higher scores typically secure better rates, potentially saving you a considerable amount over the life of the loan. To improve your credit score, regularly monitor your credit through reports from major bureaus like Equifax, Experian and TransUnion. Correct any inaccuracies immediately. Consistently paying your bills on time is crucial, as payment history is a key factor in credit scoring. Aim to reduce your overall debt, especially on credit cards, to lower your credit utilization rate. Also, avoid opening new credit lines shortly before applying for a mortgage, as this can temporarily lower your score.

Managing Your Debt-to-Income Ratio (DTI): Lenders assess your DTI ratio to evaluate your ability to manage monthly payments and repay debts. To improve your DTI, increase your income through additional work, if possible, and pay down significant debts, particularly high-interest credit cards. A lower DTI ratio makes you a more appealing candidate to lenders.

Exploring Down Payment Options The size of your down payment affects your loan's terms and whether you'll need to pay for private mortgage insurance. Building a robust down payment can be achieved by regularly setting aside a portion of your income into a dedicated savings account. Additionally, investigate state and local first-time homebuyer assistance programs, which can offer grants or low-interest loans to help with your down payment.

Document Preparation Having the correct documentation ready can expedite your mortgage application process. You will need detailed proof of income, such as recent pay stubs and tax returns from the past two years. Prepare to show your asset documentation through bank and investment account statements, which demonstrate the origin of your down payment. It's also wise to keep information about your current debts and employment verification handy, as lenders may request this data to confirm your financial stability and employment status.

By carefully managing your finances and preparing thoroughly for the application process, you enhance your chances of securing a mortgage that fits your financial situation. Each step prepares you to qualify for a mortgage and positions you to receive the best possible terms.

THE TRUE COST OF DEBT: HOW INTEREST REALLY WORKS

Understanding the mechanics of interest rates and the true cost of debt is crucial for financial planning and debt management. This section dives into how interest rates are determined, the role of compound interest, and strategies to minimize interest payments. It also provides real-life examples to illustrate the long-term impact of debt.

Understanding Interest Rates Interest rates are the cost you pay for borrowing money, determined by several factors, including market conditions, credit score, loan amount, and loan term. Lenders use these rates to assess the risk associated with lending money. Fixed rates remain the same throughout the loan period, offering predictability and protection from rate increases. However, Variable rates can change over time based on the lending market dynamics, which could either lower your costs or increase them significantly.

Compound Interest: Friend and Foe Compound interest is a powerful financial concept where interest is calculated on the initial principal and the accumulated interest from previous periods. When it comes to investments, compound interest accelerates the growth of your money over time, effectively earning interest on interest. However, when applied to debt, compound interest can significantly increase the amount you owe, making it harder to pay off your debt quickly. For instance, credit card debt, which typically uses compound interest calculated daily or monthly, can grow rapidly if only minimum payments are made.

Strategies to Reduce Interest Paid Minimizing the interest you pay on debts can lead to substantial savings and faster debt repayment. One effective strategy is refinancing high-interest debts into a loan with a lower interest rate, which can reduce monthly payments and the total interest paid over the life of the loan. Another strategy is to make more than the minimum payment on debts, particularly those with the highest interest rates. Even small additional amounts can cut down the principal faster, reducing the total interest accrued.

Calculating the Real Cost of Debt Understanding the actual cost of debt over time is essential. For example, consider a $10,000 loan with an annual interest rate of 10% compounded monthly. If you were to make minimum monthly payments of $200, paying off the debt would take nearly seven years, and you would pay more than $4,000 in interest alone. In contrast, increasing the monthly payment by even $50 could save hundreds in interest and shorten the repayment period significantly.

By grasping these concepts and utilizing strategic approaches to manage and repay debts, you can maintain control over your financial health and avoid the pitfalls of high-cost debt. This knowledge helps make informed borrowing decisions and underscores the importance of proactive debt management.

FINANCING YOUR MOVE: GRANTS, LOANS, AND OTHER RESOURCES

Relocating involves various expenses, whether for a job, lifestyle change, or other reasons. Understanding the financial assistance options like relocation grants, moving loans, and budgeting effectively can make the process smoother and more affordable. This section explores these financial resources and offers practical advice on managing the costs associated with moving.

Relocation Grants Relocation grants are funds provided by governments, employers, or non-profit organizations to cover moving expenses. These grants are particularly common when skills shortages exist in specific regions or industries, encouraging skilled workers to relocate. For example, some state or local governments offer relocation incentives to attract teachers, health-care providers, or tech professionals to underserved areas. Additionally, many companies provide relocation packages for employees transferring to new locations or highly valued new hires. These grants may cover moving services, travel costs, temporary housing, and sometimes even the down payment on a new home.

Moving Loans Moving loans are personal loans used to cover relocation expenses when other funds are unavailable. These loans are unsecured, meaning they do not require collateral but their interest rates and terms can vary widely based on your credit score and the lender's policies. Moving loans can be a sensible option if you need to move quickly for a job opportunity and do not have enough savings to cover immediate costs. However, it's crucial to consider the loan's terms and your ability to repay it based on your expected income in your new location.

Budgeting for a Move Creating a comprehensive moving budget is crucial to avoid unexpected financial strains. Start by listing all potential costs:

- **Hiring Movers or Renting a Truck:** Costs can vary significantly depending on the distance and the amount of belongings.
- **Packing Supplies:** Boxes, tape, bubble wrap, and more.
- **Travel Expenses:** Fuel, flights, hotels, and meals if the move is long-distance.
- **Insurance:** Especially if you have valuable items.
- **Storage:** If you need temporary storage during the move.
- **Settling-In Costs:** Such as deposits for utilities or new furniture.

To manage these costs effectively:

- **Get Multiple Quotes:** Shop around for the best prices on moving services and supplies.
- **Plan Ahead:** Book movers and travel arrangements well in advance to avoid last-minute premiums.
- **DIY What You Can:** Consider packing yourself or enlisting friends and family to help reduce costs.
- **Set Aside a Contingency Fund:** Unexpected costs almost always appear during a move. Having a small buffer can help you manage these without stress.

By understanding the resources available for financing your move and carefully planning and budgeting for the associated costs, you can make your relocation as smooth and cost-effective as possible. Whether utilizing grants, taking out a moving loan, or saving up, being financially prepared will help you start your new chapter on the right foot.

As you move forward, remember that choosing the right financing option is as crucial as selecting the perfect home. It involves careful consideration of your long-term financial stability and life-style needs. By applying the knowledge gained from this chapter, you are now better positioned to navigate the challenges of mort-gage financing confidently and efficiently, ensuring that your deci-sion meets your immediate needs and contributes to your enduring financial health and home satisfaction. Whether you are a first-time homebuyer or looking to expand your investment portfolio, the strategies discussed here will serve as your guide in the ever-evolving real estate market.

OVERCOMING FINANCIAL ROADBLOCKS

Success is not final, failure is not fatal: It is the courage to continue that counts.

— WINSTON CHURCHILL

Hopefully, if you've gotten this far, you feel confident and can implement some of the strategies and tips you have been reading about. If you are still questioning it and thinking, how can I come up with the money to get started or how can I save up the money to move, this chapter will help you get past some of the common hurdles and give you tools to use to make progress.

DEALING WITH UNEXPECTED FINANCIAL CRISES WITHOUT DERAILING YOUR GOALS

Navigating unexpected financial crises without compromising long-term goals requires a solid, proactive approach. This section outlines critical strategies, such as maintaining an emergency fund, embracing flexible financial planning, leveraging insurance and seeking professional advice, collectively forming a robust defense against unforeseen financial challenges.

Emergency Fund Importance An emergency fund is an essential financial safety net designed to cover unexpected expenses such as medical emergencies, sudden job loss, or urgent home repairs. This fund should ideally hold three to six months' worth of living expenses, providing a buffer that allows you to manage financial shocks without having to incur debt. Having this reserve keeps your long-term investment plans on track, as you won't need to withdraw from your retirement savings or other investment accounts, which could significantly offset your financial goals. I like to shoot to keep six months of expenses in my fund.

Flexible Financial Planning Flexibility in financial planning is crucial for adapting to life's unpredictabilities. This involves creating a financial plan and regularly reviewing and adjusting it to reflect current realities, such as changes in income, expenses and personal circumstances. Implementing flexible strategies, such as adjusting budget categories and emergency financial routes, can help you remain resilient in financial adversity. Moreover, main-taining a portion of your investment portfolio in easily liquidable assets ensures you have access to funds when you need them most, without significant penalties or losses.

Insurance as a Safeguard Insurance plays a pivotal role in safeguarding your finances against catastrophic events. Health insurance, homeowner's insurance, auto insurance, and life insurance are all designed to provide financial compensation in the event of specific losses, shielding you from potentially overwhelming out-of-pocket expenses. The importance of considering disability insurance cannot be overstated, as it replaces a portion of your income should you become unable to work due to illness or injury, protecting your financial stability and helping you maintain your financial commitments.

Seeking Professional Help During a financial crisis, professional advice can be invaluable. Financial advisors and credit counselors can offer strategic guidance tailored to your unique situation, helping you make informed decisions that protect your financial interests. These professionals can assist in restructuring debt, reallocating assets, or finding the most appropriate financial recovery strategies. Furthermore, they can provide emotional support and reassurance, making navigating a financial crisis less daunting.

Dealing with unexpected financial crises demands a well-rounded, proactive strategy that includes preparation, adaptability, protection and informed decision-making. Establishing a robust emergency fund, embracing flexible financial planning, investing in comprehensive insurance coverage and seeking professional advice can safeguard your financial well-being against sudden adversities. This approach helps manage immediate financial challenges and ensures that your long-term financial goals remain on track, reinforcing your financial stability for the future.

STRATEGIES FOR COMBATING FINANCIAL ANXIETY AND STRESS

Financial stress can significantly impact your mental health and overall well-being. Adopting strategies that mitigate this stress and maintaining financial sanity is essential. This section discusses how mindfulness, a supportive community, achievable financial milestones and mental health resources can collectively help manage and reduce financial anxiety.

Mindfulness and Financial Health Mindfulness involves being present and fully engaged with the current moment without distraction or judgment. Applying mindfulness to your financial life can help alleviate stress by fostering a greater awareness of your spending and saving habits. Techniques such as mindful budgeting—paying attention to how you allocate your money without harsh self-criticism—can create a more thoughtful and stress-free approach to managing finances. Regular practice can help you recognize anxiety triggers and develop healthier responses to the inevitable ups and downs of your financial life.

Building a Support Network Financial burdens can often feel less overwhelming when shared within a supportive community. You can find a sense of belonging and emotional support by building a network of trusted friends, family, or financial support groups. These networks offer a platform to share experiences, tips, and sometimes even resources, making financial challenges more manageable. Online forums, local meetups, and financial literacy workshops are excellent places to find and cultivate such connections.

Setting Achievable Financial Milestones One effective way to reduce financial stress is by setting realistic and achievable financial milestones. Break it into smaller, manageable tasks instead of focusing on a single overwhelming goal. For example, if your goal is to pay off a significant debt, start by targeting smaller chunks that you can tackle monthly or quarterly. Celebrating these minor victories can provide a psychological boost, reduce feeling overwhelmed and motivate you to achieve your larger financial goals.

Accessing Mental Health Resources Financial stress can sometimes require professional intervention to manage effectively. Financial therapists specialize in the intersection of financial advice and psychological support, helping clients work through the deep-seated issues that drive their financial behaviors. Additionally, counselors and traditional therapists can help address the anxiety and stress that arise from financial difficulties. Exploring these resources and educational materials focused on financial wellness can provide significant relief and practical coping mechanisms.

Combating financial anxiety and stress is crucial not only for your financial well-being but also for your overall health. By integrating mindfulness into your financial practices, building a supportive community, setting achievable goals, and utilizing professional mental health resources, you can create a balanced approach to managing your finances. These strategies help foster a healthier relationship with money, reducing anxiety and empowering you to take control of your financial future with confidence.

OVERCOMING THE PAYCHECK-TO-PAYCHECK CYCLE

Breaking free from living paycheck-to-paycheck is essential for achieving financial stability and independence. This section outlines strategies for increasing income, managing debt efficiently, budgeting for irregular expenses and utilizing financial tools to improve overall financial management. You will see some of the tools we have previously touched on but it's essential to see how they can make a difference.

Increasing Income Sources One of the most direct ways to escape the paycheck-to-paycheck cycle is by increasing your income. This can be achieved through various avenues:

- **Side Gigs:** Consider freelance work, part-time jobs, or turning a hobby into an income source. Platforms like Upwork, Etsy, or local service listings can help you find opportunities that match your skills.
- **Higher-Paying Jobs:** Continuously improving your skills and qualifications can make you eligible for higher-paying positions. Keep an eye on job openings, seek additional certifications or training, and don't hesitate to negotiate salaries to ensure you're being paid your worth.
- **Passive Income Streams:** Investments in stocks, real estate, or starting a side business can generate passive income, reducing reliance on your primary paycheck.

Prioritizing High-Interest Debt High-interest debt, such as credit card debt, can significantly hamper your ability to save and invest. Prioritizing these debts for repayment can free up more of your income each month:

- **Debt Avalanche Method:** As discussed previously, this method focuses on paying off debts with the highest interest rates first while maintaining minimum payments on others. This method saves money on interest over time, speeding up debt repayment.
- **Balance Transfers:** Consider transferring high-interest credit card balances to a card with a lower interest rate or a promotional 0% APR period. This can provide breathing room to reduce balances without accruing additional interest.

Budgeting for Irregular Expenses Irregular expenses such as annual insurance premiums, holiday gifts or car maintenance can disrupt your financial stability if not planned for.

- **Set Aside Monthly Amounts:** Break down expected annual costs into monthly savings goals and set this amount aside in a dedicated savings account.
- **Emergency Fund:** Build and maintain an emergency fund that can cover these irregular expenses without impacting your budget. This prevents the need to use credit for unforeseen costs.

Utilizing Financial Tools Leverage technology to gain better control over your finances:

- **Budgeting Apps:** Tools like Mint, YNAB (You Need A Budget), or EveryDollar can help track your spending, categorize expenses, and set budget goals. These apps often link to your bank accounts and credit cards to provide real-time financial insights.
- **Spending Alerts:** Set up alerts on your banking apps to notify you when you're approaching set spending limits or when unusual transactions occur, helping you monitor your spending habits.

Overcoming the paycheck-to-paycheck cycle involves increasing your income, strategically managing debts, planning for irregular expenses and utilizing modern financial tools to keep track of your finances. By implementing these strategies, you can start building a buffer between your costs and income. This will set the stage for greater financial security and the ability to pursue long-term financial goals without stress.

ADDRESSING AND CORRECTING POOR FINANCIAL DECISIONS

Everyone makes financial mistakes, but the key to economic resilience is learning from these errors and implementing strategies to avoid repeating them. This section covers practical steps to address and correct past financial missteps, including learning from mistakes, consolidating debt, rebuilding credit and setting safeguards for future financial decisions.

Learning from Mistakes Adopting a mindset that views mistakes as learning opportunities is crucial. Reflect on what led to the poor financial decisions: Was it a lack of information, unplanned spending, or not sticking to a budget? Understanding the root causes can prevent similar mistakes in the future. Acknowledge the error without harsh self-judgment and commit to making better financial choices.

Debt Consolidation Strategies Consolidating multiple debts into a single loan can effectively manage and correct past financial oversights. Debt consolidation simplifies your finances by combining various debts with differing interest rates into one loan, typically with a lower interest rate. This can result in easier management and potentially lower total interest costs. Options for consolidation include personal loans, balance transfer credit cards, and home equity loans. Each has its considerations, so choosing one that matches your financial situation and goals is essential.

Rebuilding Credit Scores Poor financial decisions can often lead to a damaged credit score, but there are several steps you can take to rebuild it:

- **Pay Bills on Time:** Consistently making timely payments is one of the most significant factors in improving your credit score.

- **Reduce Credit Utilization:** Keep your credit utilization ratio under 30%. This involves paying down existing debt and not maxing out credit cards.
- **Keep Old Accounts Open:** Older credit accounts contribute positively to your credit history length, so keep them open even if you're not using them frequently.
- **Limit New Credit Inquiries:** Too many hard inquiries in a short period can negatively impact your credit score. Apply for new credit only when necessary.

Implementing Safeguards To prevent future poor financial decisions, consider setting up financial safeguards:

- **Automatic Savings Plans:** Automate transfers to a savings account to build a buffer to prevent going into debt for unexpected expenses.
- **Spending Limits:** Set spending limits on your credit and debit cards to control impulse buying and ensure you stay within budget.
- **Financial Planning Tools:** Use budgeting and planning apps to track your spending and stay alert to financial habits that could lead to trouble.

Addressing and correcting poor financial decisions involves a combination of introspection, strategic financial actions, and proactive safeguarding techniques. By learning from past mistakes, consolidating and managing debt efficiently, actively working to rebuild credit and setting up systems to prevent future missteps, you can regain control over your financial health and lay a foundation for long-term financial stability.

NAVIGATING FINANCIAL CHALLENGES AS A COUPLE OR FAMILY

Managing finances as a couple or within a family can introduce unique challenges and opportunities. Effective communication, the decision between joint versus separate accounts, cohesive budgeting strategies, and managing financial inequality are all critical elements in navigating these waters smoothly. This section explores these aspects to help couples and families foster a healthy financial relationship.

Communication Strategies The cornerstone of successful financial management in any relationship is open and honest communication. Regular financial meetings can create a safe space for each party to express their views on money, discuss financial goals, and review expenditures. This proactive approach helps prevent misunderstandings and conflicts about money and reinforces mutual goals and commitments. Establishing a routine that encourages transparency and fosters trust is crucial, as it ensures both partners feel heard and valued in financial decision-making.

Joint vs. Separate Accounts Deciding between joint and separate banking accounts is a significant decision for couples.

- **Joint Accounts:** These accounts can simplify the management of household expenses, making it easier to handle bills and save for shared goals. They promote transparency and can strengthen trust, as both partners have access to the financial movements within the account. However, they also require a high level of trust and cooperation, as financial missteps by one partner can affect both.
- **Separate Accounts:** Maintaining separate accounts offers individual autonomy over personal finances, which can be crucial when partners have different spending habits or

financial philosophies. It can also provide security in case of relationship breakdowns. However, it might complicate the management of shared expenses and savings goals unless there is clear communication and a robust system of financial accountability.

Budgeting as a Team Creating a family budget involves more than just tracking expenses; it's about aligning financial priorities and setting shared goals. Start by outlining all income sources and monthly expenses, then agree on priorities like savings, debt repayment, and discretionary spending. Use tools like joint budgeting apps to track progress and hold each other accountable. Regular budget reviews help adjust goals as financial situations or priorities change, ensuring all family members stay aligned and committed.

Dealing with Financial Inequality When one partner earns significantly more than the other, it can lead to feelings of inequality or tension. Addressing this requires careful handling:

- **Equal Contribution vs. Proportional Contribution:** Couples should discuss whether expenses like rent, groceries, and savings contributions are split equally or proportionally based on income. Each method has merits, and the right choice depends on the couple's values and financial situation.
- **Transparency and Inclusion:** Regardless of income differences, both partners should have an equal say in financial decisions. Regular discussions about finances can help ensure both partners feel valued and included.

Navigating financial challenges as a couple or family requires a blend of open communication, shared financial planning, and mutual respect for individual preferences. By choosing the right strategies for bank account management, engaging in collective budgeting, and thoughtfully addressing income disparities, couples and families can build a solid financial foundation that supports both their relationship and their financial goals.

MOVING WITH KIDS: MINIMIZING STRESS AND MAXIMIZING EFFICIENCY

Relocating with children adds an extra layer of considerations and challenges to the moving process. From involving kids in the move to selecting the right time and place and utilizing helpful resources, there are strategic ways to make the transition smoother and more favorable for the whole family.

Engaging Kids in the Process Involving children in the moving process can help them feel part of the decision and ease their anxiety about the change. Allow them to participate in age-appropriate activities, such as:

- **Packing their own belongings:** Give them boxes and let them decorate and pack their room. This can help them feel in control and excited about the move.
- **House hunting:** If possible, involve older children in selecting the new home or show them pictures and videos if they can't be there in person. Ask for their opinions on potential homes.
- **Planning the room layout:** Let them decide how to set up their new room, choose new decorations, or plan the color scheme.

Choosing the Right Time to Move Timing can significantly affect how well children adjust to a move. Consider the following to minimize disruption:

- **Academic year:** Moving during the summer break or
between school years can reduce disruption to your child's
education and provide a natural break during which they
can adjust before starting at a new school.
- **Social considerations:** Consider the timing of social
activities or important events in your child's life. It might
be easier to move after a significant event like a major
school project or a social event where saying goodbye can
be more meaningful.

Finding Family-Friendly Communities Choosing the right
community is crucial when moving with children. Look for areas
that offer:

- **Good schools:** Research the local schools' performance as
a top priority. Websites like GreatSchools.org provide
ratings and parent reviews that can offer insight into the
school environment.
- **Parks and recreational facilities:** Check for nearby parks,
community centers, and recreational leagues that can
provide your children with opportunities to meet peers
and engage in activities.
- **Safety and amenities:** Ensure the neighborhood is safe
and well-equipped with necessary amenities, including
libraries, medical facilities, and grocery stores, essential for
a family's everyday life.

Resources for Families Leverage resources and services designed
to assist families during a move:

- **Moving services specialized in family relocations:** Some
companies offer services tailored to families, such as
helping set up the children's rooms first to ensure they are

settled.

- **Community resources:** Upon arrival, connect with local community centers or social services that offer programs for children and families. These can be invaluable for helping your family integrate into the community.
- **Online forums and local parent groups:** Platforms like Facebook groups or Meetup.com can provide connections with other local families who can offer advice and friendship.

Moving with children requires careful planning and consideration. Still, by involving them in the process, choosing the right timing, selecting a supportive community, and utilizing available resources, you can help ensure a smoother transition. These strategies aim to minimize the stress associated with moving and enhance your children's overall experience, helping them feel excited and optimistic about their new home and community.

REBUILDING YOUR FINANCIAL LIFE AFTER MAJOR SETBACKS

Recovering from a significant financial setback is not just about regaining lost ground; it's also an opportunity to rebuild your financial life more robustly than before. This process involves reevaluating and redefining your approach to managing money, from paying off debt to saving and investing wisely.

Starting Fresh: Embrace major financial setbacks as opportunities for a fresh start. This shift in perspective allows you to critically evaluate what went wrong and what can be learned from the experience. Begin by setting new financial goals that are clear and achievable and use these as your guiding principles to navigate your financial recovery. This proactive approach helps restore confidence and provides a structured path forward.

Strategic Debt Repayment Addressing accumulated debt requires a strategic approach. Start by thoroughly assessing all your debts, prioritizing them by interest rate and balance. Techniques like the debt avalanche or snowball methods can be effective depending on whether you're motivated by saving on interest or achieving quick wins. Additionally, communicating with creditors can lead to negotiated terms, such as reduced interest rates or extended payment plans, which make your debt easier to manage.

Re-establishing Financial Stability With a plan for your debt in place, focus next on building a stable financial base. An essential first step is establishing an emergency fund, even if contributions are initially small. Over time, this fund should grow to cover several months of living expenses, acting as a buffer against future financial surprises. Concurrently, begin to contribute to savings regularly, prioritizing consistency over quantity. As your financial situation improves, seek advice on making smart investments to solidify your financial security further.

Preventive Measures Preventing future financial setbacks involves continuous education and regular financial reviews. Stay informed about best financial practices and understand the potential risks to your financial health. Ensure you have comprehensive insurance coverage tailored to your needs, which you should review and adjust as your life circumstances change. These actions build resilience against future financial shocks and ensure you are always prepared for unexpected challenges.]

Rebuilding after a financial setback is a comprehensive process that involves more than simply recovering lost assets. It's about developing a resilient financial strategy that includes effective debt management, thoughtful investment in your future, and preventative measures to safeguard against potential risks. With determination and a structured approach, you can rebuild a more secure financial future and regain confidence in your financial management skills.

BRINGING IT TOGETHER

Navigating through financial roadblocks is essential for achieving and maintaining long-term financial stability. This chapter has equipped you with vital strategies to manage and surmount the financial challenges many individuals and families encounter. From handling unexpected financial crises with resilience to breaking the paycheck-to-paycheck cycle and correcting past financial errors, the information provided empowers you to take control of your financial destiny.

Each section has emphasized the importance of proactive financial management, whether it's through establishing a solid emergency fund, strategically reducing debt, or setting attainable financial goals. We also explored the critical role of preventive measures and ongoing financial education to help safeguard against future difficulties and ensure continuous financial well-being.

As you reflect on the lessons from this chapter, consider these questions to deepen your understanding and apply what you've learned:

1. **What steps can you take today to start building or increasing your emergency fund and how might this change your approach to financial crises in the future?**
2. **Reflect on a past financial mistake: What did you learn, and how have you adjusted your financial practices based on that experience?**
3. **Evaluate your current financial habits: What preventive measures could you implement to better protect yourself from potential financial setbacks?**

By pondering these questions and implementing the strategies discussed, you will be better prepared to face financial challenges directly, turn adversities into opportunities for growth and pave a path toward a more secure and prosperous financial future. It's the Prosperity Path!

A CHANCE TO EMPOWER OTHERS

Financial freedom is more achievable than many people realize – you just need to be fully informed about your options. This is your chance to help more people to get there.

Simply by sharing your honest opinion of this book and a little about what you found here, you'll empower more people with the knowledge they need to improve their own financial health.

JUST ONE CLICK!

Thank you so much for your support. It makes more of a difference than you realize.

Scan the QR code below

FINAL THOUGHTS

EMBRACE YOUR FINANCIAL FUTURE WITH CONFIDENCE

As we end this journey through "Personal Finance & Property Mastery Hacks," it's clear that the power to transform your financial future lies within your grasp. Throughout this book, we've explored the profound impact that financial literacy and strategic relocation can have on your financial well-being. Understanding the intricacies of personal finance and considering the financial advantages of geographic relocation can open doors to significant savings and increased income. By arming yourself with this knowledge, you are better positioned to make informed decisions that will lead to a more secure and prosperous future. Let's look at some of the key takeaways:

1. **Understanding Your Financial Health**: Knowledge is the foundation of financial success. By comprehensively evaluating your credit report, creating a zero-based budget, and building a robust emergency fund, you have the tools to take control of your finances.

2. **Tax Strategies**: Where you live significantly impacts your tax liabilities. By considering state income taxes, property taxes, sales taxes, and even local city taxes, you can strategically relocate to areas that offer significant tax savings, increasing your disposable income.

3. **Generating Income**: Your property is more than just a place to live; it's a potential source of income. Innovative use of your property, such as short-term rentals, leasing unused land, or harvesting timber, can provide substantial financial benefits.

4. **Remote Work and Geographic Arbitrage**: In today's digital age, remote work offers unprecedented flexibility. By taking advantage of geographic arbitrage, you can live in a lower-cost area while earning a higher income, maximizing your financial potential.

5. **Overcoming Financial Roadblocks**: Every journey has challenges, but you can overcome financial obstacles with determination and strategic planning. From managing debt effectively to making informed investment decisions, staying focused on your goals will lead to long-term prosperity.

6. **Strategic Relocation**: Move to areas that offer better financial opportunities and lower living costs to maximize your income and savings.

EMPOWERMENT AND ACTION:

This book has provided you with the knowledge and strategies to make informed decisions about your financial future. This book is not just a collection of economic theories but a practical guide designed to empower you with actionable steps. Each chapter has been crafted to provide clear, concrete actions that you can implement immediately. Whether it's creating a zero-based budget, exploring tax advantages, or generating additional income through property, these strategies are meant to be used as tools for your financial success. Now, it's time to take action. Consider your goals, evaluate your current situation and implement the strategies that resonate most with you. I encourage you to take the first step today. Apply the techniques from this book and witness the transformation in your life.

Remember, every small step counts. Whether you move to a new location to save on taxes, rent out a part of your home, or simply stick to a well-structured budget, each decision brings you closer to financial freedom.

A VISION FOR THE FUTURE:

Imagine a future where you have the financial flexibility to pursue your passions, support your loved ones and enjoy life without the constant stress of financial uncertainty. This vision is attainable and starts with the decisions you make today.

As you progress, keep this book as a guide and a reminder of your potential to create a prosperous and fulfilling life. Embrace the journey, stay resilient, and always seek opportunities to improve and grow.

Thank you for embarking on this journey with me. I hope the insights and strategies shared in this book inspire you to take control of your financial destiny. Remember, the key to financial success is not just in making money but in making informed, strategic decisions that align with your long-term goals.

Your path to prosperity starts now—embrace it with confidence and determination. Here's to your financial success and a future filled with abundance and opportunity!

RESOURCES

"6 Quotes to Help Motivate You to Achieve Financial Freedom." LA Financial Credit Union. Accessed July 15, 2024. https://www.lafinancial.org/6-quotes-to-help-motivate-you-to-achieve-financial-freedom/

Ten essential tips for adjusting to life in a new city. (2024, May 6). https://treasure moving.com/10-moving-to-a-new-city-essential-tips-how-to-adjust/

A beginner's guide to renting out your house - SmartAsset | SmartAsset. (2023, August 1). https://smartasset.com/mortgage/a-beginners-guide-to-renting-out-your-house

AirDNA | Short-Term Rental Data Analytics | VRBO & Airbnb Data. (n.d.). https://www.airdna.co/

Barroso, A., & O'Shea, B. (2024, April 22). How to read a credit report. NerdWallet. https://www.nerdwallet.com/article/finance/read-credit-report

Bloom, L. B. (2023, November 14). These places in the U.S. will pay you as much as $15,000 to move there. Forbes. https://www.forbes.com/sites/laurabegley bloom/2023/09/20/these-us-cities-will-pay-you-as-much-as-15000-to-move-there/

Brown, J. (2024, March 6). How to pay for moving expenses: 4 options to consider. Bankrate. https://www.bankrate.com/loans/personal-loans/how-to-pay-for-relocation-costs/

Burnette, M. (2024, May 3). Emergency Fund calculator: How much will protect you? NerdWallet. https://www.nerdwallet.com/article/banking/emergency-fund-calculator

Christenson, P. R. (2023, November 20). 13 Benefits of Financial Planning — Phillip James Financial. Phillip James Financial. https://phillipjamesfinancial.com/blog/13-benefits-of-financial-planning

Credits and Deductions | Internal Revenue Service. (n.d.). https://www.irs.gov/credits-and-deductions

Equifax. (2023). How to improve your credit scores to help you buy a home. https://www.equifax.com/personal/education/credit/score/articles/-/learn/improve-credit-score-to-buy-home/

Karl, S. (2023, December 27). Looking Back at 2023's Wild Ride for Mortgage Rates, What's In Store for 2024? Investopedia. https://www.investopedia.com/looking-back-at-2023s-wild-ride-for-mortgage-rates-whats-in-store-for-2024-8420284

Loopholes of real estate (2nd ed.) (2013). Sutton, G., ESQ. RDA Press.

Luthi, B. (2023, November 2). How to rebuild your credit. https://www.experian. com/blogs/ask-experian/credit-education/improving-credit/how-to-rebuild-credit/

McGurran, B. (2023, December 19). Avalanche vs. Snowball: Which Debt Repayment Strategy Is Best? https://www.experian.com/blogs/ask-experian/ avalanche-vs-snowball-which-repayment-strategy-is-best/

NerdWallet: Finance smarter. (n.d.). NerdWallet. https://www.nerdwallet.com/

Pelchen, L. (2024, April 16). The hidden costs of moving in 2024: people are under budgeting by $723. Forbes Home. https://www.forbes.com/home-improve ment/moving-services/hidden-costs-of-moving/

Publication 527 (2023), Residential Rental Property | Internal Revenue Service. (n.d.). https://www.irs.gov/publications/p527

Publication 946 (2023), How to Depreciate Property | Internal Revenue Service. (n.d.). https://www.irs.gov/publications/p946

Schulz, M. (2024, May 24). 49% of Americans can't afford a $1,000 emergency, with many relying on credit cards for unexpected expenses. LendingTree. https://www.lendingtree.com/debt-consolidation/emergency-savings-survey/

Sentelle, S. (2024, May 16). How to Move Cross-Country on a Budget (2024 Guide). This Old House. https://www.thisoldhouse.com/storage-organiza tion/reviews/how-to-move-cross-country-on-a-budget

Team, M. V. (2024, February 16). The financial implications of remote work on expenses and savings. YMV. https://yourmoneyvehicle.com/uncategorized/ the-financial-implications-of-remote-work-on-expenses-and-savings/

The differences between FHA, VA, and USDA mortgages. (2020, December 4). Yale, A. J., & Yale, A. J. HousingWire. https://www.housingwire.com/articles/ the-differences-between-fha-va-and-usda-mortgages/

Topic no. 414, Rental income and expenses | Internal Revenue Service. (n.d.). https://www.irs.gov/taxtopics/tc414

Topic no. 415, Renting residential and vacation property | Internal Revenue Service. (n.d.). https://www.irs.gov/taxtopics/tc415

Topic no. 701, Sale of your home | Internal Revenue Service. (n.d.). https://www. irs.gov/taxtopics/tc701

Tulsa Remote | Make Tulsa your new headquarters and home. (n.d.). https://www. tulsaremote.com/

Updater. (2024, March 21). How to transfer utilities and what you need to start, stop services. https://updater.com/moving-tips/documents-youll-need-to-start-stop-or-transfer-utility-service/

Warshaw, J. (2024, March 20). 27 Side hustle ideas to earn extra cash. Ramsey Solutions. https://www.ramseysolutions.com/saving/side-hustle-ideas

What is Zero-based Budgeting? | The Ultimate Guide | Anaplan. (n.d.). https://www.anaplan.com/blog/zbb-zero-based-budgeting-guide/

NOTES

www.ingramcontent.com/pod-product-compliance
Lightning Source LLC
Chambersburg PA
CBHW071645210326
41597CB00017B/2120